TRACING YOUR BRITISH ANCESTORS

Colin R Chapman

SECOND EDITION

With Revisions

LOCHIN PUBLISHING

This is another in the series of Chapmans Records Cameos designed for social, local and family historians world-wide. This Cameo and others in the series by the author originated as his lectures, many of which are profusely illustrated with pertinent examples. The author will, accordingly, be pleased to lecture to family history, genealogical or other societies or groups on the subject of this Cameo or other matters of interest to the social, local and family historian.

The cover by Nick Ind emphasises that British ancestors originated in England, Wales, Scotland, Ireland, the Isle of Man and the Channel Islands.

The map on page 46 is based on one kindly supplied by Manx National Heritage.

Published by
LOCHIN PUBLISHING
6 Holywell Road, Dursley, GL11 5RS, England

First Edition 1993 (1 873686 07 2)
Second Edition 1996 (1 873686 13 7)
Copyright of the Lochin Publishing Society 1993, 1996, 1999
Reprinted with revisions 1999

British Library Cataloguing in Publication Data
Chapman, Colin, 1939-
Tracing Your British Ancestors - 2 Rev. ed
(Chapmans Records Cameos Series)
I. Title II. Series
929
ISBN 1 873686 13 7

Contents

Figures

Preface

Tracing Your British Ancestors, which deals also with Irish ancestors, as explained in Chapter 1, is now well established as an important "how to" book for amateur and professional genealogists and family historians. This revised edition incorporates useful website addresses and the latest changes in the location of a number of archives holding material that you will be using when compiling your family tree or simply collecting more data in preparing your family history. Lifeboat service and light-keepers records are now mentioned. The Yorkshire Civil Registrars' records have been brought together under one roof. The old, familiar, buildings in London of Somerset House and the Public Record Office in Chancery Lane are but mere memories of past affection holding, or in some cases withholding, information on our ancestors. But the records themselves are, in the majority of cases, even more accessible than before, though the repositories may now be in, as yet, unfamiliar places. On a cheerful note, hosts of indexes and finding aids are available nowadays, many on CD-ROM or the Internet, to help us more easily locate those irritating ancestors who are not baptised, are never at home on a census night, who marry someone from another county, and who appear to die and be buried when on a journey far from home - or at least far from where we consider they ought to have been.

Since the publication of previous editions of this Cameo, the names of many British counties and their boundaries were changed yet again, in a rolling programme from 1996, and one county, Rutland, dissolved in the 1974 re-organisation, has been resurrected. Many new unitary authorities, in most instances having similar status to a county, have been formed, while other counties such as Avon, created by the 1972 Local Government Act which came into force in 1974, have been dispersed into new, or incorporated into old, areas. In this edition I have again concentrated on the pre-1974 situation, the counties where your ancestors resided and worked; in many cases the records themselves have not been moved although the name of the archive office may be slightly different. For information, I have included some maps of the positions of counties before and after 1974. Maps of the Anglican Church's dioceses in England and Wales appear in my Cameo *Ecclesiastical Courts, Officials and Records: Sin, Sex & Probate*. Parish maps of the Isle of Man and of Guernsey and Jersey in the Channel Islands, and even the locations of all of these islands, are also included in this Cameo as not a few of my readers have told me that such information would be helpful.

Apart from the above changes, most of my remarks prefaced to the first edition of this Cameo remain relevant. Were I a 19th Century writer, I would invite you, gentle reader, to take delight in my opening remarks again, even should you have had the good fortune to read them hitherto. And to you, dearest new reader, I also address a cordial invitation to peruse these my opening comments, together with my ensuing text, confident in the knowledge that you will soon be in fellowship with friends whose acquaintance you will be obliged to acknowledge that you find it both a joy and a delight.

I began tracing my British ancestors some fifty or more years ago with help from family and friends, professionals and amateurs; and I have been lecturing on British genealogical research and British social and family history for thirty years or so. On many occasions my audiences world-wide asked why I hadn't, before now, written a book in the Chapmans Records Cameo series on tracing British ancestors.

My response was generally that there were books already in print on the subject. "But not," my audiences insisted, "with fascinating details, those extra snippets of information that you weave into your presentations". And many such books on British material made only passing references to Scottish and Irish research and have often totally ignored the Isle of Man and the Channel Islands.

This book attempts to redress the balance and to include a host of useful and fascinating facts, whilst taking you, the ancestor-hunter, by the hand through some of the sources available. Where sources or their backgrounds have been sparsely covered elsewhere, I have devoted more space to them in this book; adequately-covered material I have mentioned less liberally.

As with my other Cameos, I have provided useful addresses and suggestions for further reading where you may discover additional information. Whilst beginners may need guidance, I do not believe that any serious family historians amongst you want to have it all provided "on a plate" - and if I included every aspect of the subject here, the book would be too thick and you wouldn't read it anyway!

Genealogists and family historians will debate forever the correctness of their titles. In many parts of the world the term "family historian" is applied to a person researching only one family surname - conducting a one-name study, some would say - whilst others imply there is only one family historian in any family - the poor (or rich) individual who has the custody of all that family's archives. Some family historians concentrate on the social and cultural histories of all their ancestors - their positions in the local community and their occupations or trades, details on their houses and other possessions, their crops and so on. Others claim that genealogists prepare only boring pedigrees or family trees whilst family historians produce vibrant chronicles of their ancestors. But I have met thousands of lively genealogists and have read some pretty boring family histories. Accordingly, I have tended in the following chapters to use genealogy and family history as synonyms, to avoid giving you, kind reader, any particular tag - apart from realising that, for whatever motive, you are interested in tracing your British ancestors.

There are almost no records in the British Isles which have been kept especially for genealogical purposes - apart from those associated with Royal or noble families where inheritance of wealth, land and title was of paramount importance. The armorial achievements (coats of arms) associated with such families were recorded by heralds from the College of Arms, who were and still are members of the Royal Household.

For all other "ordinary" families from whom I, and many of you, are descended, genealogical information has to be found in archives originally kept for totally different purposes - normally by the Church or the Monarch or Government of the day. Such archives are housed centrally or locally, depending on whether the original legislation which caused the records to be maintained was centrally required by the Church or enacted by the Crown or national government, or locally enacted in the counties, in the regions or in the parishes. The Established Church in the British Isles, Roman Catholic until the Reformation in the 16th Century and Protestant (Anglican) after then, originally kept some records centrally and its local records in the dioceses, archdeaconries and parishes.

In general today both secular and spiritual records are housed together - but filed quite separately. National and provincial civil and ecclesiastical archives are held in General Registries, Public Record Offices and National Archives; local government and diocesan, archdeaconry and parish archives are held in the appropriate regional and county record offices. There are, in addition, many other specialist archives - for example the records of the ecclesiastical Province of York at the Borthwick Institute of Historical Research at York University, some records with regimental archives and museums, some Nonconformist church records in their own historical societies' archives and most university college records at the colleges themselves. Nevertheless, the regional and county archives contain important records which are extremely useful and valuable to you in tracing your British ancestors.

I would be arrogant, however, if I claimed to be the sole authority on the records I have described in the following chapters. My colleagues within the Federation of Family History Societies and from the Society of Genealogists have offered me wonderful opportunities to share research methods and experiences; Member Societies have invited me to speak throughout Great Britain and the Channel Islands, enabling me to visit scores of local and national archives. Many county and diocesan archivists have opened treasure chests in their record offices for my delight. There was the ministry of my parents over a period of forty-five years in pursuing this obsession (it is no longer a hobby) and the encouragement of my friends, particularly Kevin and Nick for their tolerant support, in spite of still regarding ancestor-hunters as eccentric; and Jim, whose ancestors always tumble effortlessly out of every register and off every tombstone - a paradigm for you all. Pauline Litton, yet again, has offered copious suggestions, many of which I have accepted with gratitude.

But most of all I must thank my ancestors - without them neither I nor this book would have been possible.

COLIN R CHAPMAN

Chapman County Codes for British Isles Areas

Aberdeenshire	ABD	Dyfed	DFD	Lincolnshire	LIN	Shetland Isles	SHI
Alderney	ALD	East Lothian	ELN	London	LND	Shropshire (Salop)	SAL
Anglesey	AGY	East Riding Yks	ERY	Londonderry (Derry)	LDY	Sligo	SLI
Angus (Forfar)	ANS	East Sussex	SXE	Longford	LOG	Somerset	SOM
Antrim	ANT	England	ENG	Lothian	LTN	South Glamorgan	SGM
Argyllshire	ARL	Essex	ESS	Lothian, East	ELN	South Yorkshire	SYK
Armagh	ARM	Fermanagh	FER	Lothian, West	WLN	Staffordshire	STS
Avon	AVN	Fife	FIF	Louth	LOU	Stirlingshire	STI
Ayrshire	AYR	Flintshire	FLN	Man, Isle of	IOM	Strathclyde	STD
Banffshire	BAN	Forfar (Angus)	ANS	Manchester, Greater	GTM	Suffolk	SFK
Bedfordshire	BDF	Galway	GAL	Mayo	MAY	Surrey	SRY
Berkshire	BRK	Glamorgan	GLA	Meath	MEA	Sussex	SSX
Berwickshire	BEW	Glamorgan, Mid	MGM	Merionethshire	MER	Sussex, East	SXE
Borders	BOR	Glamorgan, South	SGM	Merseyside	MSY	Sussex, West	SXW
Brecknockshire	BRE	Glamorgan, West	WGM	Mid-Glamorgan	MGM	Sutherland	SUT
Buckinghamshire	BKM	Gloucestershire	GLS	Middlesex	MDX	Tayside	TAY
Bute	BUT	Grampian	GMP	Midlothian	MLN	Tipperary	TIP
Caernarvonshire	CAE	Greater Manchester	GTM	Monaghan	MOG	Tyne & Wear	TWR
Caithness	CAI	Guernsey	GSY	Monmouthshire	MON	Tyrone	TYR
Cambridgeshire	CAM	Gwent	GNT	Montgomeryshire	MGY	Wales	WLS
Cardiganshire	CGN	Gwynedd	GWN	Morayshire	MOR	Warwickshire	WAR
Carlow	CAR	Hampshire	HAM	Nairnshire	NAI	Waterford	WAT
Carmarthenshire	CMN	Hereford & Worcester	HWR	Norfolk	NFK	West Glamorgan	WGM
Cavan	CAV	Herefordshire	HEF	North Riding Yks	NRY	West Lothian	WLN
Central Region	CEN	Hertfordshire	HRT	North Yorkshire	NYK	West Midlands	WMD
Channel Islands	CHI	Highland Region	HLD	Northamptonshire	NTH	West Riding Yks	WRY
Cheshire	CHS	Humberside	HUM	Northern Ireland	NIR	West Sussex	SXW
Clackmannanshire	CLK	Huntingdonshire	HUN	Northumberland	NBL	West Yorkshire	WYK
Clare	CLA	Inverness-shire	INV	Nottinghamshire	NTT	Western Islands	WIS
Cleveland	CLV	Isle of Man	IOM	Offaly (Kings)	OFF	Westmeath	WEM
Clwyd	CWD	Isle of Wight	IOW	Orkney Islands	OKI	Westmorland	WES
Cork	COR	Ireland	IRL	Oxfordshire	OXF	Wexford	WEX
Cornwall /	CON	Jersey	JSY	Peebles-shire	PEE	Wicklow	WIC
Cumberland	CUL	Kent	KEN	Pembrokeshire	PEM	Wight, Isle of	IOW
Cumbria	CMA	Kerry	KER	Perthshire	PER	Wigtownshire	WIG
Denbighshire	DEN	Kildare	KID	Powys	POW	Wiltshire	WIL
Derbyshire	DBY	Kilkenny	KIK	Queens (Leix)	LEX	Worcestershire	WOR
Derry (Londonderry)	LDY	Kincardineshire	KCD	Radnorshire	RAD	Yorkshire	YKS
Devon	DEV	Kings (Offaly)	OFF	Renfrewshire	FRW	Yorkshire, East Rdg	ERY
Donegal	DON	Kinross-shire	KRS	Roscommon	ROS	Yorkshire, North	NYK
Dorset	DOR	Kirkudbrightshire	KKD	Ross & Cromarty	ROC	Yorkshire, North Rdg	NRY
Down	DOW	Lanarkshire	LKS	Roxburghshire	ROX	Yorkshire, South	SYK
Dublin	DUB	Lancashire	LAN	Rutland	RUT	Yorkshire, West	WYK
Dumfries & Galloway	DGY	Leicestershire	LEI	Salop (Shropshire)	SAL	Yorkshire, West Rdg	WRY
Dumfriesshire	DFS	Leitrim	LET	Sark	SRK		
Dunbartonshire	DNB	Leix (Queens)	LEX	Scotland	SCT		
Durham	DUR	Limerick	LIM	Selkirkshire	SEL		

[Also see the maps on pages 20, 24, 30 and 46]

1. British Ancestors?
English? Welsh? Scottish? Irish?

If your ancestors were any of these, or perhaps from the Isle of Man or the Channel Islands, then this book is for you. Over the years, all of these groups have been called British, although today some of the inhabitants of England, Wales, Scotland, and Ireland and their cousins overseas, may have very different ideas of their nationality. But you are interested in your ancestors and you do not have to get involved in today's politics or nationalistic opinions here. Nevertheless, you should understand how the various parts of the British Isles are correctly described, even if this upsets some politicians and nationalists. Genealogists and family historians can look at history objectively and you need not let subjective ideals rule your mind while you trace your ancestors.

Wales and England were formally united in 1535 although Wales had been annexed to the English Crown from 1284. Many Statutes and formal documents mention only England (to the horror of the Welsh) even though applying to England and Wales. Scotland (occasionally termed North Britain) was a separate Kingdom until the Act of Union between England (and Wales) and Scotland created Great Britain in 1707 - although the English and Scottish Crowns had been united in 1603. Ireland joined the trio in 1801 to form the United Kingdom of Great Britain and Ireland until 1922, when the United Kingdom of Great Britain and Northern Ireland was formed.

Each of the countries within the United Kingdom today issues its own postage stamps but those of one country are valid in the others. All countries within the United Kingdom use a common currency, sterling, although some banks in Scotland and Northern Ireland issue their own bank notes which are legal tender in the remainder of the United Kingdom (even if some shop assistants initially look askance at unfamiliar paper money).

In Ireland, twenty-six counties in the south of the island separated for political reasons from the six northern counties in 1922 to form the Irish Free State governed from Dublin. The six counties were termed Northern Ireland which remained in the United Kingdom. The Irish Free State changed its name to Eire (from the ancient name, Erin, for Ireland) in 1937 and to the Republic of Ireland in 1949 when it left the British Commonwealth and Empire. Also termed the Irish Republic or Southern Ireland it is today regarded as a separate country with all which that involves. However, it was probably a part of Britain in the times of your ancestors who may have been termed British by some authorities, even themselves, though Irish by others.

The Isle of Man and two bailiwicks, Guernsey and Jersey, in the Channel Islands are British Crown Dependencies - all have their separate parliaments and civil registration systems, issue their own currencies and postage stamps, not valid in the

United Kingdom - although United Kingdom currency, but not United Kingdom postage stamps, is accepted on those islands. For certain purposes, taking censuses and defence for example, the Isle of Man and the Channel Islands are considered with the United Kingdom. Indeed, for genealogical research there are enough similarities in their archival records for them to be considered in this book with those from elsewhere in the British Isles.

The traditional languages of the different parts of the British Isles were English (throughout), Welsh (in Wales), Scots and Gaelic (in Scotland and parts of Ireland), Irish and Erse (in other parts of Ireland), Manx (on the Isle of Man) and French (or a variation of French) on the various Channel Islands. Some of the older records that you need to refer to may be written in these languages, although it is likely that the official, and certainly the national, government records will be in English and, prior to 1733, probably in Latin.

If you believe that your ancestors came from any of the countries or islands which at one time or another have had links or an association with any parts of Britain, read on - the following chapters will help you in Tracing Your British Ancestors.

The Channel Islands, England & France

[Also see the maps on pages 20, 24 and 30]

2. Beginning the Hunt

Civil Registration of Births, Marriages and Deaths

When tracing your ancestry, your family history or your genealogy, you should always work backwards in time. This will apply wherever you are now living in the world; whether your ancestors never left the British Isles, or whether they left a few hundred years ago and settled elsewhere. The best point to begin in tracing your British ancestry is with yourself.

It is probable that you know your date of birth, even if you do not remember your parents, but you may not have been told where you were born. In the past, this might have caused a problem; however, these days just about every country is so bureaucratic that some government department is bound to have required that your birth was registered, although this may have been a while after you were born. Since the 19th Century in the British Isles, when a birth was registered, a certificate was provided by the registrar showing information given at the time of registration.

England & Wales - general

In England and Wales, the civil registration system began on 1 July 1837. Parents are given 42 days to register a birth, after which late registration incurs a financial penalty - although it was not compulsory to register a birth until 1875. After six months, registration is not strictly possible; hence you will find some birthdates being "modified" by informants to comply with the letter of the law. In 1836 England and Wales were divided into Registration Districts, each having a local Superintendent Registrar of Births, Marriages and Deaths.

As an aside, you may like to know that these Registration Districts were based on the Poor Law Union areas resulting from the 1834 Poor Law Amendment Act, explained later in Chapter 9. Once every three months the English and Welsh local registrars sent copies of their records to the Registrar General in London for his clerks to compile quarterly national alphabetical indexes of births, of marriages and of deaths. Elsewhere in the British Isles, apart from Ireland (see below), the indexes in various styles were compiled annually. This, or a similar system of registering important events with a government or provincial or state official, is known in some countries as the Vital Records.

Scotland & Ireland - general

Civil registration began in Scotland on 1 January 1855, although there is a series of registers of Neglected Entries of births, marriages and deaths from 1801 to 1854, compiled in and after 1855 of some individuals who were not recorded in church registers (see Chapter 6). In Ireland civil registration began on 1 January 1864, although there had been a registration system for marriages, where one or both parties was Protestant, from 1 April 1845. From 1 January 1922 copies of civil registration records in the Irish counties of Antrim, Armagh, Derry (Londonderry),

Down, Fermanagh and Tyrone, then being in Northern Ireland, were forwarded to the Registrar General in Belfast. For the remaining Irish counties, then being in the Republic of Ireland, copies of civil registration records continued to be sent to the Registrar General in Dublin.

Isle of Man & Lundy Island - general

On the Isle of Man civil registration of births and deaths was introduced in 1849, but was not made compulsory until 1878; civil marriage registration for Dissenters was made available from 1849. Anglicans continued to use existing parish marriage registers (see Chapter 6) although many parishes opened new register books in 1878. The Douglas Registrar was appointed Superintendent Registrar for all of the Isle of Man in 1924. The General Registry in Douglas holds the civil registers and annual indexes of births, marriages and deaths for the whole island, microfilm copies are in the Manx Museum Library, Douglas; their addresses are given in Appendix 1.

Births from 1865 to 1869 on Lundy Island in the Bristol Channel - a traditional smugglers' haven - were recorded and indexed in a separate volume by the Registrar General of England and Wales in the Overseas Registers series.

Channel Islands - general

In the Channel Islands civil registration of births and deaths for Guernsey, Herm and Jethou began in October 1840, and of non-Anglican marriages in January 1841. Marriages solemnized by the Anglican Church were not registered with the civil authorities until 1919. The civil registration of births, marriages and deaths on Sark and Alderney until 1925 was maintained by the local registrars on those islands and after then by the Registrar General on Guernsey. Some of the Alderney civil registers disappeared during the German occupation of the Channel Islands between 1940 and 1945: the birth registers, for example, prior to 3 August 1850 no longer exist; for marriages and deaths see below. All the civil registration registers for Guernsey, Herm, Jethou, Sark and Alderney, with indexes, are held by the Registrar General on Guernsey. Copies of the 19th Century records are held in the Priaulx Library, St Peter Port, Guernsey. Some of the indexes are by islands, some by parishes, others are alphabetical annually for groups of islands; e.g. the annual indexes for births and for deaths on Alderney plus Sark from 1925 and alphabetical indexes of births for Guernsey, Herm and Jethou from 1840 by surname and then date. Some records of Germans who occupied the Channel Islands in the 1940s are in Guernsey, others are in Germany.

For Jersey the civil registration system was introduced in August 1842. Prior to 1948, births, marriages and deaths could be registered in French or English. Be aware that births of French nationals were registered at the French Consulate. The original registers of births and deaths and non-Anglican marriages are held by the parish registrars; the marriage registers of Anglican marriages are held by the clergy. Access to the indexes to registers of births, marriages and deaths is through the Superintendent Registrar for Jersey who holds the parish index volumes (there are no consolidated indexes for Jersey). La Société Jersiaise (see Appendix 1) has a special arrangement with the Superintendent Registrar for access to the indexes.

Birth Registration

It is useful to remember that in England a person's full name was traditionally a surname (the family name or father's surname) and one or more Christian names (personal or first names, formally given to an individual at a Christening or baptismal service in a church). In Wales the traditional system was for a person to have their own (Christian) name clarified by adding that of their father - so that Thomas Williams was really Thomas, son of William. David, the son of Thomas Williams would be known as David Thomas and his son Rees, would be known as Rees Davies. However, as the 19th Century progressed, the English tradition of a surname with one or more Christian names was used also in Wales. In England and Wales, in Scotland and for the Isle of Man and the Channel Islands, two types of birth certificate are available:

a) a short certificate, signed by the registrar; this shows the full name of the child, the date of birth and the registration district where the birth was registered.

b) a full certificate, signed by the registrar, and showing the full name and sex of the child, the date, and sometimes the time of birth (the normal practice in Scotland - in England it often signifies multiple births, twins or more), the place of birth, which in a city or town may have the house number and the name of the street; there will also be the full name of the mother, including her maiden surname, the full name and occupation of the father, the name (sometimes only a surname and initials) of the person registering the birth, the date of registration and the registration district in which the birth was registered.

Since 1963 certificates for births (and marriages and deaths) registered in Wales have been issued on bilingual forms for events taking place both before and after 1963. The original certificates, however, for events in Wales prior to 1963 were printed only in English. So your Welsh ancestors from 1837 to 1963 would have been offered certificates only in English, even if the copy you obtain today has headings in English and Welsh. More than a few Welsh births were not registered at all, particularly in remote areas, the parents believing that a baptism or infant dedication in a Nonconformist chapel met the requirements for civil registration. So if you cannot find a Welsh birth in the civil records, try looking in the Church records, in case your ancestors had this misunderstanding.

Birth certificates, and other civil registration certificates for events in England and Wales may be purchased from the Registrar General. From 1837, for the English and Welsh events, the alphabetical indexes of all the births, like huge phone books, were compiled every three months or quarter of a year until 1984. From 1 January 1984, all the births for a whole year are in an annual index. Both the quarterly, and after 1984 the annual, indexes are available for free inspection at the General Register

Office in the Family Records Centre, London (see Appendix 1); but they are only indexes to the certificates and you have to purchase copies of the certificates themselves to obtain the names on them which you need for your family history. However, you can glean some genealogical information from the 20th Century birth indexes because from the third quarter (July, August and September) of 1911 they show the mother's maiden surname. The quarterly indexes have been filmed, and the microfilms or microfiches bought by libraries all over the world. So you may be able to look through these indexes without having to travel to London.

From the index entry you should note the year, the quarter, the name of the registration district and all the reference numbers and letters. You can then order a copy of the appropriate certificate from the General Register Office. Note that a different address (see Appendix 1) is used for postal applications. It is also possible, if the exact date and location of the event is known, for you to obtain a certificate by writing to the local Superintendent Registrar of the district in which the event was recorded. Local registrars do not use the same reference numbers and letters which are in the Registrar General's indexes, so it is of no help for you to quote those if you do contact a local registrar. You should also be aware that most local registrars, unlike the Registrar General, do not have a public search room or any facilities for you to search through the local indexes yourself.

In Scotland, the Registrar General's records are kept at New Register House, Edinburgh (see Appendix 1) where you can access the indexes via a computer terminal which is extremely "user friendly". Having paid a fee, all you have to do is indicate that you are looking for a birth, the sex of the baby, the year, the surname and the initial of the first name. The screen then offers a choice of individuals which you can narrow down by successively adding the full name, the registration district where you believe the birth was registered and the mother's maiden surname. You are even offered a choice of spellings for the names, and of years of birth around the year you indicated. The screen then gives a reference for you to look at microfiche copies of the Registrar General's original registers, from which you can make notes or buy certified or uncertified (and cheaper!) copy birth certificates. If the computers are not available you can search through the indexes, as in England.

The Scottish indexes were compiled annually (not quarterly as for England and Wales) and arranged alphabetically under males and females for the whole of Scotland. The birth indexes, from 1929, include the mother's maiden surname. Having found a possible index entry you should look through the microfiche copies of the registers and either make notes or buy a birth certificate. Even without the computer you will be able to do the research more quickly than elsewhere in the British Isles (apart from, perhaps, Guernsey), and also collect more genealogical information from each registered entry; furthermore, you do not have to make so many initial assumptions when doing your searches. Very many Scottish records are available on the Scots Origins pay-per-view website <http://www.origins.net>.

As mentioned above, since 1 January 1922 the Irish civil records of births, marriages and deaths for what is now the Republic of Ireland, have been held by the Registrar General at Joyce House, Dublin with the civil records prior to 1922 for the whole of Ireland. The civil records from 1 January 1922 for what is now the province of Northern Ireland are held by the Registrar General at Oxford House, Belfast. The information on the certificates for Northern Ireland is similar to that for England and Wales. In the birth indexes in the Republic of Ireland, for which you will have to pay a fee to gain access at Joyce House, the mother's maiden surname first appears in 1900. In Ireland the index volumes from 1864 to 1877 are annual, but after then are quarterly as in England and Wales; but there are additional comprehensive alphabetical indexes to births for the period 1864 to 1877, and for the Republic of Ireland from 1966 to 1987. In Northern Ireland you will also have to pay a fee at Oxford House to look at the indexes, which are again annual after 1973.

You may search through the indexes for the Isle of Man in the General Registry, Douglas; for Guernsey, Herm, Jethou, and for Sark and Alderney before 1925 look in the indexes at the Royal Court House at the States Office, Guernsey (see Appendix 1), but for Jersey you will have to write to the Superintendent Registrar who will do the searches for you.

You can appreciate that in tracing your ancestors, full certificates, with information on at least one parent - the mother - are going to be much more useful to you than short certificates. Look at your own birth certificate and see what information that gives you. If you have only a short certificate or an equivalent document, then you should order a full birth certificate to obtain more information about your parents. If you were adopted when you were younger, it may be that you have assumed the surname of your adoptive parents, and you may have only an adoption certificate at the moment. In England and Wales it is now possible to obtain your original birth certificate if you were adopted.

You may find a blank in the space for the father's name or occupation; or the certificate may state "not known". This is a possible indication that the parents were not married at the time of the birth of the child. The identity of the father will have to be found from other sources, or may never be discovered; but that is a situation which we shall briefly mention in Chapter 9. If the father's name does not appear on the certificate, the child normally assumes and later uses the mother's surname, although this is not always the case.

In Scotland a birth certificate in 1855 and from 1861 shows even more information than a full certificate for England and Wales or Ireland; the Scottish system required the informant to tell the registrar the date and place of the parents' marriage (on the assumption that there was one!). For 1855 (only) Scottish birth certificates also show the ages and places of birth of the parents and details of any of their previous children.

Marriage Registration

Having obtained the birth certificate, your next step is to obtain the parents' marriage certificate (assuming the parents were married). Throughout the British Isles, civil registration marriage certificates have been available since the 19th Century. In Scotland this step should merely require you to take the date of marriage from the birth certificate, and from that use the computer or the annual indexes to find the appropriate record of the civil registration of the marriage. For England and Wales, Ireland, the Isle of Man and the Channel Islands, assume initially that the birth certificate is for the oldest child and that the parents married at around the time of the birth of that child.

Depending on where the event took place i.e. England and Wales, Ireland etc., you will have to look through the appropriate marriage indexes either at the Family Records Centre or Joyce House Dublin, Oxford House Belfast, the General Registry Douglas, or the Royal Court House Guernsey (or on microform copies of the indexes) to locate the name of, say, the mother which you obtained from the birth certificate. For Jersey events you have to write to the Superintendent Registrar. Of course, it is possible that the child on the birth certificate (and that could be you) is the youngest of fourteen children. That is a nuisance in your hunt, though not a major problem, but it does mean searching back through many more index volumes until the names of the parents can be found.

At the Family Records Centre, for entries prior to the last quarter (October, November and December) of 1911 you should note the details as you did for a birth certificate; then look in the marriage index of the same quarter for the name of the father which you also obtained from the birth certificate. At Joyce House, you have to follow this procedure for marriages before 1966. If the reference numbers and letters for the marriage index entries are the same, you have probably got the right couple and you can apply for their marriage certificate. Beginning in March 1912, an entry in the marriage indexes of the brides at the Family Records Centre for England and Wales (and from 1966 in the annual indexes at Joyce House) includes the bridegroom's surname, and an index entry for the bridegroom shows his bride's maiden surname, which makes the searching a little bit easier. In the Scottish marriage indexes the spouses' names appear from 1929, although from 1855 to 1863 the groom's surname was included beside the bride's name in the indexes of brides.

A marriage certificate for England and Wales, the Isle of Man and the Channel Islands, gives the date and place of the marriage, the name of the person who conducted the ceremony and what form it took, the full names of the bride and the groom, their addresses and the ages that they told the registrar they had at the time, their marital conditions (bachelor, spinster, widow etc.), their occupations, and the full names and occupations of the fathers of both of them. Channel Islands marriage certificates additionally, most helpfully, state the birthplaces of the bride and groom. As in the case of a birth certificate, a marriage certificate shows the registration district in which the event took place. A blank or a "not known" in the column for the name or occupation of the father may indicate that the bridegroom or the bride were illegitimate, or that the father died when they were children and they really didn't know his name or occupation. There may be a note beside the father's name that he is "deceased"; but be aware that the absence of such a note does not signify that he was alive at the time of the marriage of his off-spring.

The registration of marriages in Ireland from 1845 required the dates of birth of the bride and groom (not merely their ages), their marital conditions, the names and maiden names of their mothers (but not their fathers' occupations) and their intended future residence; unfortunately, however, the certificates normally show only the same details as for England. Remember that from 1845 to 1863 only marriages to a Protestant spouse were registered. This information was also required from 1864 for all Irish marriages. The Scottish registrars, in addition to the information required in England and Wales, asked the bride and the groom for the full names of both parents (not of just the fathers), the maiden surnames of the mothers and, from 1855 until 1922, any relationship between the bride and groom. In 1855 Scottish registrars also asked for the birthplaces of the bride and groom and details of any previous marriages of both parties, including any children resulting from such marriages. All this information was put on the marriage certificates for that year.

On the Isle of Man, although the Registrar General was appointed in 1849, Anglican marriages continued to be registered in the parish churches until 1878 or later. However, the Manx General Registry holds indexed copies of the earlier parish registers, so you can research the records there as if they were civil registers. In the Channel Islands from 1919, a marriage could take place in any Anglican church, any place of worship licensed by the Royal Courts for marriages, the offices of the Registrar General at the Greffe on Guernsey, or the Superintendent Registrar on Jersey, or in any private dwelling house in the presence of the Registrar General. The civil marriage registers for Alderney survive only from 1 July 1891.

From the information you get on a marriage certificate - the full names of the bridegroom and the bride, and their ages - you can then look again at the birth registration indexes, this time to locate the references to enable you to order the birth certificates of the previous generation. One word of caution here: at their marriage a bride and groom often (and particularly in the Channel Islands until 1919) told the registrar or officiating minister that they were "of full age", which meant anything over 21 (20 in the Channel Islands) until 1978, since when in the British Isles full age has been over 18. So you could have a long search if the couple were in their nineties, and you believed them to be in their twenties; although some common sense and normal child-bearing ages should be taken into consideration in your calculations.

You should also be aware that the partners were not always truthful in declaring their ages, and of course the information on the certificate reflects what the couple said, not necessarily the correct ages. It was quite common in the Victorian era for the bride to be slightly older than the groom, although at that time this was not thought "proper". You may find, therefore, that the bridegroom "adjusted" his age upwards and the bride brought hers down by a year or so, just to make their marriage more acceptable.

With this in the back of your mind, you can continue the procedure, from certificates of birth, to those of marriage, to birth, to marriage, and so on, back to the beginnings of civil registration. It will take time to achieve this, because for each event in England and Wales a separate certificate has to be ordered, and it may take a week or more before you receive each one. But this process will, in theory anyway, enable you to get back to 1837 in England and Wales, 1864 or possibly 1845 in Ireland, 1849 on the Isle of Man and 1840 or 1842 in the Channel Islands. Whilst in Scotland your searching may be accomplished more quickly, you can go back only to 1855 using the statutory registers of the civil registration system.

The converse of marriage, its annulment, divorce or separation, was an extremely complex process in England and Wales prior to 1857 - normally through a Private Act of Parliament or by finding a flaw in the legality of the marriage to demonstrate it was somehow invalid. Petitions for divorce from 1668 to 1857, through Private Acts, are indexed in the House of Lords Record Office (see Appendix 1). Since the 1857 Matrimonial Causes Act, civil courts have been able to pronounce on divorce in England and Wales. Brief records of decrees absolute (names of husband and wife, date, and sometimes place, of marriage and date of decree) from 1858 to the present are in the Principal Registry of the Family Division at First Avenue House, Holborn, London (see Appendix 1). These records are not indexed by names, nor open for general inspection although, for a fee, you may write for some information. Alternatively, you may be able to find details on divorces from newspaper reports. The Public Record Office (PRO) at Kew holds the divorce court books (1858-1882) [J170] and files with petitions for decree and nullity (1858-1948) [J77], indexed from 1858-1958 [J78]. From 1938 only a selection of files has been kept; at the PRO you are able to look at indexes and some records over 30 years old - see Appendix 1 for the address. Divorce in Scotland has been possible since the Reformation. Divorce in Ireland was not possible until 1995. Considerable detail on divorce and related records throughout the British Isles is given in the Cameo *Marriage Laws, Rites, Records & Customs* (see Appendix 2).

Death Registration
You can also glean further information on your ancestors from the civil registration death records - their dates, places and causes of death, and the ages the informant believed them to be. Deaths, as for births and marriages, were required to be reported to local registrars, who forwarded details to the Registrar General. When this system was introduced in England and Wales a death should have been registered within eight days, although from 1875 the time was reduced to five days.

Quarterly indexes, similar to those for births and for marriages, have been maintained since their introduction. For England and Wales, after December 1865, the reported age at death was included in the indexes; after March 1969 the actual date of birth, if known and given to the registrar, has been included in the indexes, instead of the age.

An Irish death certificate shows for the deceased, the date and place of death, the full name, sex, marital condition, occupation, cause of death and duration of illness, and the signature, qualification and residence of the informant, as well as the date when the death was registered and the signature of the Registrar. All the Irish death indexes include age at death; and since 1966 have included the marital condition of the deceased.

Death entries in Scotland may be inspected at New Register House, as in the case of birth and marriage entries, and they also provide more information than certificates issued in England and Wales; a Scottish registrar asked the informant for the time of death, the names of the parents and the spouse or previous spouse of the deceased; if these were known they were included on the death certificate, so providing you with facts that may take considerably longer to uncover in England and Wales. For 1855 a Scottish death certificate also included the birthplace of the deceased and the length of residence in the district prior to death. From 1855 to 1861 the place of burial and certification by the undertaker were also shown on the death certificate. The annual death indexes for Scotland from 1866 include the age of the deceased (as in the case of England and Wales). From 1973 the maiden surname of the deceased's mother also appears in the annual indexes.

On the Isle of Man compulsory registration of deaths began in 1878, although there are a few 1877 deaths registered. A death certificate gave the same details as on an English or Welsh certificate until 1970, when residence and date and place of birth were included, also as for England and Wales from this time. Indexes of deaths for the Isle of Man have been compiled annually since 1878 and included the age at death until 1980. The indexes are available for public search at the General Registry and as copies at the Manx Museum.

Death certificates from the Registrar General on Guernsey give for the deceased, the date, hour, place and cause of death, the full name (for a married woman, her maiden surname and also her husband's full name), the age and place of birth, occupation and usual residence, the full name of the father and mother and also the maiden surname of the mother. After 1907 the name of the doctor certifying the cause of death was also included. Prior to 1949 married women were indexed only under their maiden surname. Until 1963, deaths for Guernsey, Herm and Jethou were indexed alphabetically by parish, but an alphabetical listing by surname and then date of death has been maintained since then. Deaths on Alderney and Sark from 1925 are indexed separately in the Registrar General's office, although the local registrars hold the civil registration death registers from 2 August 1850. Jersey death certificates have the same information as English and Welsh death certificates.

The Registrars General also hold indexes to some Miscellaneous Registers of births, marriages and deaths of British subjects which occurred out of the British Isles. Examples at the Family Records Centre (which are also available on microfiche in some libraries), are Consular Births (1849-1965), Consular Deaths (1849-1965), Deaths at Sea (1837-1965), Deaths in the Air (1945-1965). From 1965 these events have been recorded together as Births and Deaths Abroad (1966-the present). In the miscellaneous series are also events (relating to British subjects only) in Overseas Registers for which there are separate indexes for Holland (1627-1894), India (1894-1947), Portugal (1814-1876) and Russia (1840-1918), to quote only four examples from nearly 20 countries.

In the General Register Office in Edinburgh are Consular Returns of births, marriages and deaths (from 1914), some earlier registers from certain foreign countries, Marine Registers (from 1855) and Air Registers (from 1948) of births and deaths, for persons who were specifically identified as from Scotland. The Scottish Registrar General also holds the registers of Neglected Entries mentioned above.

What you should do next

Over the weeks or months that you are gathering information from the Registrars' records, there are at least two other avenues that you should be exploring, before delving into the next set of records, described in Chapter 5.

In the first of the two other avenues there is a great deal of information you can discover from those of your own family who are still alive; in the second avenue there may be someone who is also doing research on your family. Chapters 3 and 4 look at ways you can investigate these aspects. You could also have a quick look, now, at Chapter 14, to pick up some ideas on organising the information you are beginning to accumulate. In Chapter 5 we shall return to some official, government, records to continue the hunt.

3. Family Sources - for free!

What do your relatives know?

Initial questions among immediate family members may suggest that no one remembers, or wants to remember, anything; "the past is best forgotten", "I threw all that stuff out ages ago", "they were a funny lot anyway, particularly on your granny's side", or "I can't think why you want to drag up all that now, times have changed". But those are probably some of the reasons why you DO want to find out more about your ancestors and your family history. So do not be discouraged by early rebuffs, and keep on asking; and try looking in cupboards, drawers, the spare room or the loft for scraps of information that have been tucked away around your home, or at your parents', or grandparents' or aunts' or cousins' homes. With luck, it will not all have been thrown out, and you may discover stacks of information that has been forgotten for years.

Items "accumulated" at home

You may come across copies of birth, marriage and death certificates; which is another reason for looking around before you spend too much money on further copies from the civil registration authorities. You should look out for newspaper cuttings, birthday books, diaries, scrap books, letters, photograph albums, pension books, military service records, passports, graduation certificates, school prizes and reports, many of which have dates of birth, or other significant events recorded on or in them. Wedding invitations in the form of bidding letters in some parts of the British Isles, particularly Wales, and death notifications in the form of memorial cards, may have survived from the Victorian and Edwardian eras. You may even discover the old Family Bible with noteworthy family events written at the front, or between the Old and New Testaments, or at the end.

Copies of newspapers and specialist journals, not just the cuttings you find at home, in local and national collections, often provide contemporary reports and opinions not available from official documents; the booklet *Using Newspapers & Periodicals* gives the range and whereabouts of these British publications and discusses their value to family historians. *Family History in Focus* by Don Steel deals with using photographs in genealogical research. We look in more detail at military records in Chapter 11. One of the Cameos in this series, *The Growth of British Education and Its Records*, is devoted to the amazing amount of family history and genealogical information available from school, college and university records. See Appendix 2 for details on all these titles.

In addition to your "two-dimensional" finds, you may discover artifacts that give details on your family members - school attendance or prize medals, cups for growing the largest turnip or achieving the highest skittles score, an apprentice's work piece, military medals or decorations, a silver salver or pewter tankard to commemorate a retirement or an engraved watch as a long-service award, all with names and dates. You may not be able to take these items away with you, but you could photograph them, or at least copy the inscriptions.

Contacting relatives

It is certainly worth your while talking to the older members of your family, and making notes of what they tell you, however insignificant it may appear. A piece of apparently irrelevant information, even gossip, may just provide that vital clue you need later on. Some people make the effort to record on audio or video tape what their relatives can tell them; but a few folk clam up when a cassette or camera is produced. So you will just have to use some common sense about methods that are acceptable and useful for you to dig out memories and family stories. You may find that several visits to certain members of your family is the best way to slowly recover the details, especially if the person supplying you with this information has not had cause to dwell on it for several decades. After a bit of practice, you will develop a style that elicits masses of information even from relatives who initially claimed to have nothing at all with which to help you.

You may not be able to visit your relatives in person, and you may have to rely on telephoning or writing; in these days of electronic communication, you may prefer to send a fax or e-mail or use other methods of data transfer.

Before rushing to the phone, or even visiting, jot down the information you need and ask it in a logical order. If you are writing via fax or e-mail, or even using good old-fashioned note-paper, posting your letter for air-mail or surface-mail transmission, you will obviously have time to compose your questions. Over the phone, or beside a person, it is easy to become enchanted with the stories when they do flood out, and you may even forget to prompt your relative into remembering the vital facts you are seeking. Do not worry if they cannot recall immediately the exact date of a birth or marriage or death; they may be able to link it with other events - "just before the Coronation" or "between the wars" or "on Independence Day"; you may need to do some supplementary reading to pinpoint the actual year or month, but you'll pick up some history on the way.

Nicknames

Most families use nicknames or familiar names for their children and brothers and sisters; names which were quite logical choices at the time, but may not be so obvious a couple or more generations later. Some individuals were never referred to by the names under which they were registered or baptised. "There was your Uncle Jack - his real name was John", "Great Aunt Polly fell off a pony - she was actually Mary Ann". Write down what you are told and sort it out later. My father was registered as Ernest Donald Chapman but known as Don all his life. I was registered as Colin Richard Chapman but invariably referred to by my parents' generation, until I was well into my forties, as "Little Ernie" (after my father's first name which he never used for himself!); all very clear for us, but no doubt will lead to confusion in years to come.

Family legends

Do not be surprised that tales from your relatives refer to your forebears being wealthy landowners, or successful business folk or a factory manager. But do not be disappointed in your later research when you discover that the name of the factory was correct, but your ancestor was a storeman, not the manager. Ancestors often have a knack of being promoted posthumously by their descendants! On the other hand there is almost always a grain of truth somewhere in a tale, the factory name for example, and so you should record everything you are told - it will eventually fit somewhere into the jigsaw.

British Isles "Counties" pre-1974
[The Chapman County Codes are on page 4]

[The Orkney and Shetlands Isles and the Channel Islands are not shown. Also see the maps on pages 24, 30 and 46]

4. Subscribed/Registered Research

Who Else is Researching Your Ancestors?

Years ago, as mentioned in the Preface, only the gentry, nobility and royalty made careful notes of their ancestry; although the bards in Wales, like the Maoris in New Zealand, encouraged oral genealogy. They taught their youngsters to learn and recite from memory genealogies stretching over decades, even centuries. Nowadays, however, many researchers from all social, economic and political persuasions are prepared, even anxious, to tell anyone and everyone of their research - the surnames (family names) in which they are particularly interested and for which areas and periods of time. There are several areas, described in the next few paragraphs, where this "telling" takes place; you should try to consult these - you may find a distant cousin you had lost, or did not know even existed. Or perhaps a researcher has studied a particular location and undertaken an extensive local history project on its individual inhabitants, including your ancestors. In case you think this may take the fun out of your hunt, if someone else has "done it first", do not forget that no serious historian (including genealogists and family historians) believes anyone else; all "facts" provided by others should be checked by going back to the original records, or at least microform copies of originals, wherever possible.

"Upper class" biographies

For those who aspire to the gentry, the nobility or royalty, there are well-known reference works such as *Burke's* or *Debrett's* or the *Complete Peerage* and various *Baronetages* and works on Titled and Landed Gentry; from the late 18th and throughout the 19th Centuries there were very many similar works. Most of the older public libraries, in their reference collections, have a good selection of these books of "the knobs". But be warned here, as well. Just because detail is in print there is no guarantee that it is flawless. A few 19th Century genealogists, who provided the pedigrees that have become incorporated into reference volumes, must have had vivid imaginations on occasions. There are some relationships in those printed works for which there is no evidence whatsoever.

Local histories

Several county histories, including the many volumes of the *Victoria County History*, incorporate pedigrees and histories of influential families for the respective counties. Some local and parish histories often contain biographical notes on local personalities, some of whom may be connected with your family. Most county historical record societies publish at least annual volumes many of which are "people-oriented". It is certainly worth while browsing through the indexes in these, and in the more comprehensive county histories - you never know when an ancestor may pop up. The major reference and local history libraries in each county should hold copies of these works for their areas.

Heraldic genealogies

The College of Arms - where the Heralds have their offices (see Appendix 1) - has vast collections of pedigrees. These are private collections of the Heralds and so are not available for public examination. For a fee the Heralds may search their records on your behalf. The relationship between heraldry and genealogy and even a humble family history is outlined in Chapter 13. You should be encouraged by knowing that many families moved up and down between social classes over a few generations, and so the Heralds' records may prove useful, regardless of where your family now sits.

Pedigree collections

The Society of Genealogists (SoG) has an extensive collection of British pedigrees, birth briefs and family trees; these have been deposited, since 1911, with many thousands of reference works and other records, in its Members' Library (see Appendix 1). The library is open free to members of the Society, and to the public on payment of a fee. The Society also publishes a quarterly *Genealogists' Magazine* which includes the surnames being researched by members who have submitted their interests in recent months.

Genealogical directories

Many local, national and international genealogical directories, family finders, family registers and directories of members' interests have been published, containing surnames of individuals and families being researched by those submitting the names. Some are published annually, or less often, as books, in microform or on CD-ROM by commercial organisations and regional and county family history and genealogical societies (see Chapter 12).

The Federation of Family History Societies (FFHS) publishes a massive *British Isles Genealogical Register (BigR)* which you may find useful. Most local societies also publish, in their quarterly journals, the surnames with areas, even parishes, that their members are researching, or are prepared to help others with. You should really scour all these publications before leaping into, or writing to, the archives on a solitary mission. You may like to consider joining one of the local family history or genealogical societies; even if you cannot attend their meetings, normally held monthly, you can be linked to other members - perhaps some of them your own distant cousins - through their regular journals.

Most regional and county-based genealogical and family history societies in the British Isles belong to the Federation of Family History Societies. (The societies in Scotland have a Scottish Association of Family History Societies.) Among the many services provided by the Federation (see Chapter 12 for further details of the activities of this umbrella organisation) is the publication of a list of its Member Societies with addresses of their secretaries. This is available on the Internet or by post from the Federation Administrator on receipt of a self addressed envelope and UK postage stamps or two International Postal Reply Coupons, available from post offices around the world. The Federation's *Current Publications by Member Societies* (Appendix 2) identifies some societies which have published directories of members' interests. If you write to the appropriate societies you will discover if they can assist in locating who else is researching the same names that you are.

Advertisements about the commercial genealogical directories appear from time to time in family history journals such as *Family Tree Magazine* and *Family History Monthly* (see Appendix 2). The Society of Genealogists' Library holds copies of most of these. Copies of the Mormon (LDS) Family Register are available on CD-ROM at many of its Family History Centres; the indicators against the entries in its *International Genealogical Index* (see Chapter 6) may help you to discover who submitted the original data for "your" individuals.

Gaining from the work of others

You may save a lot of time and effort by locating someone who has devoted the last twenty or more years to research on your family. When you write, the enclosure of a self-addressed envelope, and the return postage as well with your query, is bound to endear you to your correspondent.

You may find it easier to make contact via the Internet. This has many user-groups; details on genealogy and family history throughout the British Isles can be found at <http://www.genuki.org.uk>. Of course, you should (tactfully) check what your contacts have done, so the romance of handling original sources need not be lost - and you may pick up some useful clues. You may even make contact with a distant cousin who has a photograph of your great great grandfather, which has survived on their side of the family, but has been lost from your side. It is always possible that you already know more about the family than the person or persons you have got in touch with via a directory - but then you can help them or perhaps enlist them to assist you in further research.

British Isles "Counties" post-1974
[The Chapman County Codes are on page 4]

[The Orkney and Shetland Isles and the Channel Islands are not shown. Changes introduced from 1996 are not identified. Also see the maps on pages 20, 30 and 46]

5. Census Returns

Where Did They Come From?

On the birth, marriage and death certificates that you obtain from the Registrars General or their colleagues, you will find addresses at which your ancestors claimed to be living (or dying) when those events took place. With the other information that you have been collecting from the family or other researchers (or even without their help) you will hopefully now be in the middle of the 19th Century or even earlier. Now you need to go back before the opening of the civil registrars' offices.

National censuses

National censuses have been undertaken in most parts of the British Isles every ten years from 1801, in Ireland from 1821, (apart from 1941). In fact there have been very many lists of names of individuals compiled for one reason or another throughout the British Isles since 1086 - as is very colourfully explained and detailed in the Cameo *Pre-1841 Censuses and Population Listings in the British Isles* (see Appendix 2). There was no requirement for the information from the ten-yearly (decennial) censuses to be centrally collected or collated until 1841; thus the survival and whereabouts of the 1801, 1811, 1821 and 1831 British returns vary considerably - as also explained in the Cameo referred to.

However, the censuses for England and Wales, the Isle of Man and the Channel Islands from 1841 onwards, taken household by household, by houses, by streets and by registration districts, are now the responsibility of the Office for National Statistics (ONS), formerly the Office of Population, Censuses and Surveys (OPCS). The returns are available for public perusal after 100 years. The enumerators' original returns [HO107, RG9, 10, 11 et seq. series] have been microfilmed and are available in a variety of locations, such as the Public Record Office. The addresses for this and other archive repositories are in Appendix 1. The majority of county record offices have microform copies of the returns for their areas. The National Library of Wales, Aberystwyth, has copies of the Welsh returns.

The Scottish decennial returns are kept at New Register House, Edinburgh and the 100 year rule applies there as well. The Irish censuses for 1821, 1831, 1841 and 1851 were almost all destroyed in 1922. Those that survived, mostly for 1851, are now in the National Archives in Dublin. The 1861 and 1871 censuses were officially destroyed by a court order, although a few returns or copies of returns appear to have escaped destruction. Some compensation for the loss of 19th Century returns may be found in the Tithe Applotment and Griffith Valuation surveys (see Chapter 10). The returns for 1901 and 1911 for the whole of Ireland are available for public perusal. Subsequent censuses were taken in the Republic of Ireland in 1926, 1936, 1946, 1951, 1956, 1961, 1966, 1971, 1979, 1981, 1986, 1991 and 1996 - although some of the returns for later years are not yet open to the public. The censuses of

Northern Ireland since 1931 have followed the pattern for the remainder of the United Kingdom.

Microfilm copies of the Isle of Man census are in the Manx Museum Library; those of the Channel Islands are in the libraries of Les Sociétés Guernesiaise and Jersiaise and in Jersey Public Library. In 1971 the States of Guernsey took over responsibility for conducting their censuses and implemented a policy that thereafter census returns would be destroyed and only the results retained. For example, for a census taken on 25 April 1976 on Guernsey, Herm, Jethou and Lihou, only the analysis has survived.

Census indexes and directories

You should be aware that the censuses were taken on a geographical basis for government statistical purposes; there was no intention to locate individuals, and so no indexes of names were ever officially required or made. There is no equivalent to the American *Soundex* or *Accelerated Indexing Systems* (*AIS*) and no government-sponsored indexing programme. However, in recent years, many county and local family history societies have indexed the 1851 census returns for their areas. A nation-wide project to index the 1881 census was also undertaken by volunteers in conjunction with family history societies; this was published on microfiche and CD-ROM. Local societies, who can be contacted through the relevant county archivist or the Administrator of the Federation of Family History Societies (see Chapter 12), can advise on the availability of census indexes.

On the other hand, in the 19th Century, and even earlier, to satisfy the requirement to locate individuals at the time, some enterprising individuals and firms produced contemporary commercial, court, private and street directories - *Kelly*, *Pigot*, *White* and *Slater* and many others covered a number of areas of the British Isles. Other professional directories and biographical dictionaries were published of clergy, physicians, engineers, architects, lawyers and of every conceivable profession and trade and are extremely useful indexed collections of names.

Census information

The information requested in 1841 for England and Wales, the Isle of Man and the Channel Islands was the full names of householders and other individuals in that household, and their ages to the nearest five years, rounded downwards; so a person of 34 is listed as 30, someone of 36 as 35; under 15 the actual age is normally given. Also requested were occupations and if born in the same county as the present residence, indicated by Y (Yes) or N (No), although S (Scotland), I (Ireland) and FP (Foreign Parts) were used by some enumerators. Similar information was requested in Scotland. In Ireland individuals were required to state their dates of marriage, whether they could read or write and which relatives had died since the 1831 census. Unfortunately most Irish returns for 1841 have not survived.

The 1851 and later returns for England, Wales, the Isle of Man, the Channel Islands and Scotland, hold more useful information for your family history. Not only are individuals listed by households, but their relationship to the head of the household is given, as are their actual ages (or to be more correct, the age they gave the enumerator), their occupations and if they had an infirmity such as being deaf, blind or dumb and even the opportunity to identify if they were idiots. In Ireland they were also asked to state their religious affiliation. But equally importantly for your genealogical research today, your ancestors were asked where they were born. This information can be most illuminating or quite tantalising: the nearer to the residence on the night of the census, the more precise were the addresses of the birthplaces. For the 1851 census of Northampton, for example, a person born in the town would have their birthplace recorded by the name of one of the five parishes in the town; but for those living in Northampton and born in a London parish, the return may simply state "London", or even worse, "Middlesex".

Do not despair if for a birthplace only a city or county or country is quoted in, say, 1851. In 1861 or 1871 a fuller address may be given. You should also be conscious that when the bride and groom came from different areas, but lived near to the groom's home, a bride was likely to return to her parents' home for the birth of her first child. So the place of birth of the eldest child, may indicate the mother's place of origin if that (or indeed, she) is missing from the census return - and that detail, in turn, may help locate a missing birth certificate, if after 1837 for England & Wales, 1855 for Scotland etc.

Let us assume that the enumerator who called at your ancestor's home had you in mind when he requested and recorded the details. Get out one of the birth, marriage or death certificates that you have acquired and note the addresses which your ancestors gave. Now turn to the address in the decennial census nearest in date to that on the certificate. With luck, one of your ancestors will be at that address and you can see the place of birth. You may be even more fortunate in discovering a parent, and even a grandparent (all identified with names, ages, relationships to each other, occupations and places of birth). If you find some relations aged 60 or more in the 1851 census, you are now back into the 18th Century with their birthplaces - let us hope an identified parish, not merely a named city, county or country.

The census may further help you to piece together your family history, as well as assisting you in going back with your family tree or lineage charts. Look again at the census returns: your ancestor may have had 13 or more brothers and sisters; if each of those had a similar number of children who all survived (unfortunately not so likely a century or more ago) and they all had their own children, then it is no wonder that today you are bound to have some cousins, somewhere around. Besides being able to compile family group sheets and draw up family trees, with all the uncles and aunts and siblings on page after page, you will discover from the census returns the trades and occupations pursued by all your relatives - yet more information about their lives and times.

Census dates

You may like to know the dates on which the 19th Century and later censuses were conducted in the British Isles. Officially the returns should indicate who was at the address at midnight on the date identified, and even those on barges and on ships in harbours were listed; some returns surprisingly include people who slept in barns on census night. But inevitably, as is the case today, some people, hopefully not your ancestors, were missed off the records. From 1801 to 1831 midnight of Monday/Tuesday was chosen; from 1841 Sunday/Monday.

10 March 1801	31 March 1901
27 May 1811	2 April 1911
28 May 1821	19 June 1921
30 May 1831	26 April 1931
6 June 1841	1941 no census taken
30 March 1851	8 April 1951
7 April 1861	23 April 1961
2 April 1871	25 April 1971
3 April 1881	5 April 1981
5 April 1891	21 April 1991

The censuses were taken on the above days throughout the British Isles, apart from Scotland from 1841 to 1881 when they were one day later. Irish censuses began in 1841 on the above days; after 1922 they were taken in the Republic of Ireland on midnight Sunday/Monday of 18 April 1926, 26 April 1936, 12 May 1946, 8 April 1951, 9 April 1961, 18 April 1971, 5 April 1981 and 21 April 1991; less detailed enumerations were also made on 8 April 1956, 17 April 1966, 1 April 1979, 13 April 1986 and 28 April 1996.

Pre-1841 "censuses"

At the beginning of this chapter, a very brief mention was made of many lists (quasi-censuses) of names of individuals being drawn up from 1086. Both Church and State from time to time collected information from communities throughout the British Isles, as a basis for taxing individuals or households to raise revenue, or to discover who was suitable for being enlisted into the militia, or who was (or was not) attending church services, or merely to ascertain the size of a particular community for planning or statistical purposes.

At various different times taxes were imposed on numbers of windows, numbers of fireplaces or hearths, numbers of horses, sheep and dogs, the value of property, and the amount of hair powder used on your wig. Poll Books, Burgesses' Lists and Electoral Registers were compiled of those entitled to vote. The clergy drew up visiting lists with names of their parishioners. Easter offerings and parish collections were taken to help the needy of other parishes who had suffered fires or flooding - the resultant subscription lists have in many cases survived and so can be used by you in broadening your collection of data on your ancestors. The reasons for many of these population listings with named individuals and the circumstances under which the lists were compiled are explained in the Cameo on Pre-1841 Censuses, referred to above. You are encouraged to study that Cameo to make full use of those early "censuses" in tracing your British ancestors. In Chapter 10 we shall look at other aspects of these listings.

Going further back

From the information on census enumerators' returns you can now go back even further, to the birthplaces of your ancestors. Before 1837 there was no civil registration of births, marriages and deaths, but the Established Anglican Church kept records of baptisms, marriages and burials, and it is to those that we must now turn. Do not worry if you believe that your ancestors were not Anglican and were Jews, Roman Catholics, Quakers or other Nonconformists. Details on Nonconformists of all beliefs are given in Chapter 8. However, except for Quakers and Jews every valid marriage, until 1837, had to be conducted at an Anglican Church ceremony, except from 1653 to 1660 during the Interregnum; but we shall explain all about this and the use we shall make of parish registers in the next chapter. So read on...

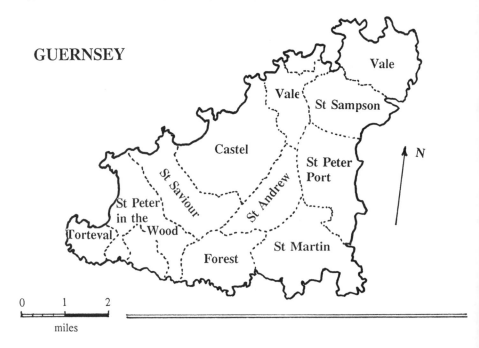

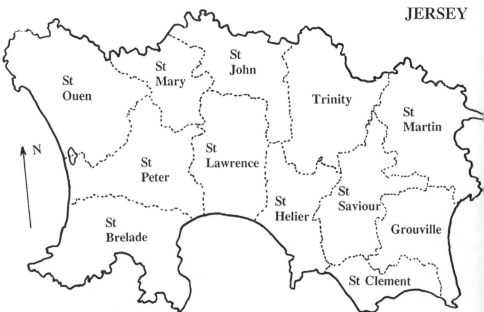

Guernsey and Jersey Parishes

[See the map on page 6]

6. Parish Registers and Transcripts
Records of Baptisms, Marriages and Burials

If you refer to the entry for your ancestor (let us assume he was William Robins) in the 19th Century census returns, you may discover that his age in 1851 was quoted as 63 and his birthplace is stated as Wellingborough, Northamptonshire. Although Wellingborough is a large town today and had a sizeable population in 1851, in 1788 it contained only one Anglican parish with a single parish church. (We shall outline the situation of other denominations generally, not just for Northamptonshire, in Chapter 8.) Turning to the register of baptisms for Wellingborough in 1788 you may find nothing, but in 1789 there is your ancestor being baptised on 7 July as William, son of William and Elizabeth Robbins. You may be tempted to discount this William because his parents' name is spelt with two bs.

You will soon appreciate that whilst today many folk are very concerned that their names are spelt in a particular way, our ancestors did not worry at all - in fact they probably couldn't read anyway, and it was usually left to the clergyman to write down a person's name as it sounded to him. So if he was new to an area and unaccustomed to local names, or perhaps a little deaf, and if your ancestors had colds or dropped their hs, or even added them or other consonants, their names could end up being spelt quite differently from document to document.

Looking back through the baptisms for Wellingborough parish you may find earlier children of William and Elizabeth Robbins (or Robins) being baptised in 1787, 1785 and the earliest in 1783. You should now follow the same procedure as when you used civil registration certificates: look in the marriage registers, working backwards from 1783. You may be fortunate to find, for example, that William Robbens (note the spelling change, again) married Eliza Pinnock on 3 April 1782. But where are these parish registers and what exactly are they? Indeed, what is a parish?

Church administrative structures

Until the 16th Century the official Christian faith throughout the British Isles was based on Roman Catholicism headed by the Pope. In 1521 Henry VIII wrote a pamphlet against the teachings of Luther, for which the Pope awarded him the title of Defender of the Faith (Fid. Def.); nevertheless, catalyzed by his marriage problems and growing pressure for Reformation throughout Europe, in 1534 the King declared himself Head of the Anglican Church, thereby separating from Rome and establishing the Protestant Anglican Church. Apart from one or two hiccoughs later in the 16th and 17th Centuries, this situation has persisted to today with the Anglican Church being the Established Church and the reigning monarch its titular head.

It could be said that at this point the Reformation hit the British Isles with the subsequent births of the Church of England, the Church in Wales (very much later -

in fact 31 March 1920), the Episcopal Church of Scotland, and the Church of Ireland, all following Anglican principles, although the Church of Ireland was disestablished in 1869. The Church of Scotland was founded on Presbyterian principles following the 1560 Scottish Act, although from 1610 to 1638 and 1660 to 1689 bishops were briefly involved. In reality the seeds of reformation had been sown earlier and they took several decades to mature. However, as the former Roman Catholic administrative organisation of the Church in the British Isles functioned reasonably well, that was more or less retained and it was the doctrinal issues that were reformed. Notwithstanding, these changes were unacceptable to some (who remained Roman Catholic) and insufficient for others (dissenting Nonconformists), as detailed in Chapter 8.

From earliest times Christian missionaries made an enormous impact on British life: the Church organised England and Wales into two provinces, Canterbury in the south and York in the north, each governed by an archbishop. All of Ireland was assigned to the province of Armagh. The Archbishop of Canterbury was (and is) the senior Archbishop and the ecclesiastical head of the Anglican Church. All three provinces were divided into a number of dioceses, each one governed by a bishop; in each diocese a cathedral, a large church, was built to hold everyone from the diocese who needed to meet on special occasions.

The Isle of Man was included in York Province, although the Bishop of Sodor and Man was fairly autonomous. The Channel Islands, initially under the Bishop of Coutances, were later within Winchester Diocese in the Province of Canterbury. Those places in the British Isles that have cathedrals were traditionally termed cities, irrespective of their populations; (although Oxford and Cambridge, because of their ancient and special university links, also became cities in their own right).

All dioceses were divided into archdeaconries, headed by archdeacons. Archdeaconries were divided into rural deaneries and those were divided into parishes in which a parish church was built and at which services were conducted by a clergyman who could be a vicar, a rector or a perpetual curate. The differences between these three originally depended on how they derived their income and how they had been appointed. Until the 19th Century many vicars and rectors lived away from their parishes, and some clergy were nominally responsible for several parishes. Some parishes had both a vicar and a rector and there may also have been an assistant curate, especially for a non-resident vicar or rector. The clergy, often called incumbents, cared not only for the spiritual lives of their parishioners but also for their several other material, social and educational needs.

The size of a parish was determined almost entirely by the number of parishioners (the population its incumbent could serve); hence in a rural sparsely populated area, a parish could cover very many square miles, whereas a town could be divided into several geographically small but densely populated parishes, each with its own parish church. An incumbent was ordained by a bishop at a special service, which in effect provided him with authority to conduct the various rites and ceremonies of the Church. He was assisted in his parish by a number of lay persons. Some of those persons, such as the Parish Clerk and one or two churchwardens (who, like other lay persons, normally received no remuneration for their efforts) were chosen by the incumbent. Others, such as additional churchwardens, were chosen by the parishioners. Some posts were held for a year, others were for life and many had to be approved by the archdeacon or the bishop. Records of these appointments were kept in the parishes or in the bishops' diocesan archives. We shall discuss in Chapter 8 the records generated by the churchwardens in carrying out their duties.

Parish registers

To better manage his new reformed Church, Henry VIII required from 1538 that in each parish in England and Wales the clergy should record, in books kept specifically for this purpose, every baptism, marriage and burial performed in their parishes. This system began hesitantly in 1560 in Scotland. Not until 1634 were the clergy required to keep registers in Ireland; and even then not many did, until the 1790s when a new Archbishop of Armagh took over. Registers in some Isle of Man parishes began in 1606 and in some Channel Islands parishes in 1560.

The value to you of the parish register entries may be beyond being able to discover the date on which your ancestor was baptised, married or buried: there is often some genealogical information, as in the case of the Robins family in Wellingborough; the names of the parents and occupation of the father of the person being baptised (although parents' names were not specifically required until 1603), the parishes of residence of the spouses being married, and the status, and sometimes the age, or the description "infant", of the person being buried. For example, "Charles, son of Joseph Clayson stonemason and Mary his wife, was baptised 1 April 1830". "William Thompson of this parish and Mary Kilborn of Cottingham were married after banns 31 August 1752". "Frances Vialls, widow, buried 15 October 1683". The names of godparents should also have been included in all baptismal registers from 1555 but, as this requirement emanated during the reign of Catholic Queen Mary I, most clergy unfortunately ignored it!

In most parishes one register book was used to record baptisms, marriages and burials; baptisms were often written at the front, marriages about half-way through, and then the book was turned upside-down and burials written in from the back. Some clergy entered in events all over the place; registers were relatively expensive and every available space was used, irrespective of the order. Occasionally, in one place in a register, all the baptisms, then marriages, then burials for one year appear without a break in a similar hand, indicating that the events were recorded, not as they occurred, but at the end of the year, probably from memory and so are subject to errors and omissions. In some of the Welsh parishes, the cost of register books was too much for the parish to afford and so they did not bother with them at all, comments to this effect appearing in later registers; even in those parishes that had registers, several incumbents failed to record the required events - a very sad situation for you today. The National Library of Wales will be able to tell you if registers were maintained in the Welsh parishes of interest to you.

If you are looking at copies of registers, hopefully (but unfortunately not always) someone else has sorted out the random order of the original entries, and has retrieved the marriages from amongst the baptisms and burials and put them into a chronological order. If you are doing your own research from the originals or from microform copies, do look at every page of early registers - just to make sure you haven't missed an entry. From the mid-18th Century successive Acts made the keeping of parish registers more orderly. Registers with numbered pages should have been used from 1711, but this was rarely done. Lord Hardwicke's 1753 Marriage Act stipulated registers for marriages; from 1813 George Rose's Act required separate printed registers for baptisms, for marriages and for burials, and a further Marriage Act required yet another layout for marriage registers from 1837. Thus your research hopefully becomes much easier in the later registers. For further details on marriage registers and other records read the Cameo *Marriage Laws, Rites, Records and Customs* (see Appendix 2).

From time to time, such as in 1694, 1695 and 1783, the government attempted to raise revenue, usually to fight the French or the Dutch, by taxing births, baptisms, marriages or burials, or the registrations of these events or the paper or parchment on which the records were made. As paupers were exempt from this tax you may discover an entry in a register with "poor", or "pauper" or "P" against the name of your ancestor. This could indicate that your ancestor was a pauper, or perhaps that he persuaded the incumbent to record him as such, so that he didn't have to pay the tax. We shall look further into pauper records in Chapter 9. Just to confuse us, some clergy used "P" to indicate that the tax had been paid, and in some burial registers "P" signifies that the person died from the plague!!

To boost the wool trade an earlier national law of 1666 required all corpses to be wrapped in a woollen cloth or shroud before being buried. An entry in a burial register stating "in woollen" or "in wool" signifies that this requirement was met. In some parts of the country separate affidavit books were kept, especially from 1678 to 1775, indicating that a burial in woollen had taken place. This Act was repealed in 1814 - although the practice of burial in wool had generally ceased before this.

Marriages were conducted by an ordained clergyman, either after the calling of banns or after the granting of a common licence by a bishop or archbishop, or a special licence by the Faculty Office of the Archbishop of Canterbury. Some marriage registers indicate which procedure was used - "after banns", "by licence", "by Lic", or simply "L" can sometimes be found alongside a marriage entry. In some parishes separate Banns Books were used which you may be able to find with the parish documents. The bond or the allegation associated with a marriage licence may also have survived and now be deposited in the appropriate county or diocesan archive. Occasionally you will find this material in the records of a Church Court, particularly if there had been a dispute at the time about the marriage. For details on how the licences were issued and under what circumstances, read the Cameo *Ecclesiastical Courts, Officials and Records* (see Appendix 2). In England and Wales after 1836, a Superintendent Registrar could also issue a marriage licence, enabling a marriage to take place where otherwise banns would have had to be published. The actual marriage may be recorded in a parish register. Many marriage licences and the associated documents have been transcribed and published. County archivists can advise you on what is available or refer to the Gibson Guide on this (see Appendix 2).

Bishops' Transcripts
By 1597 it was realised that while some incumbents were writing parish registers, others were not; and even in the cases of those who were, the ecclesiastical authorities appreciated that a single copy was vulnerable. Accordingly it was decreed that on every Sunday the incumbent, with assistance from the churchwardens, should make a transcript of baptisms, marriages and burials performed in the preceding week; and on New Year's Eve he should send the copy through his archdeacon to his bishop for safe-keeping in the diocesan registry. These copies, therefore, became known as Bishops' Transcripts (BTs) or Parish Register Transcripts (PRTs). In some areas the Archdeacon kept the copies and so these have become known as Archdeacons' Transcripts. In Ireland copies of parish register entries, known as Parochial Returns, were made in the 19th Century by some clergy, but there are no BTs as such. There are also no BTs for Scotland, the Isle of Man or the Channel Islands. However, in 1906/7 the Manx Civil Registrar called in all registers from the parish churches, copied them by hand and produced indexes to all entries. On the Channel Islands copies of the registers had been similarly made in the mid-19th Century and retained by the Civil Registrars. Since 1849 copies of Channel Islands' register entries have been sent annually to the Registrars.

It may be useful at this point to note that New Year's Eve has been on 31 December only since 1752 in most of the British Isles (Scotland had changed in 1600); prior to then it was on 24 March. Thus the New Year began on 25 March (Lady Day) and dates in records reflect this. Not all countries, even in Europe, made this change from the Julian to the Gregorian Calendar in 1752, some, like Scotland, changed earlier, some not until the 20th Century.

For us, who are using the registers several generations later, the decision to regularly generate transcripts was most fortunate: in some areas the original parish registers have been lost or destroyed by damp, rats or even incumbents or their wives. In other areas the parish registers have survived but the BTs are missing from diocesan registries. The BTs were filed according to the whim of the diocesan registrar: in some dioceses the BTs for all parishes in a rural deanery or archdeaconry or even for the whole diocese were filed together - another file was used for the following year and other files for subsequent years; in other dioceses all annual transcripts for one parish were put in one file, and all annual transcripts for other parishes were kept chronologically in their own parish files.

Whereabouts of registers

For safe keeping, parish registers, and subsequently almost all documents referring to parochial administration, were stored in the parish chest - a strong wooden trunk which for security had locks; the incumbent had the key to one lock and the churchwardens had the keys to the second and, in some cases, third locks. It was, therefore, necessary for more than one person to agree to open the chest to gain access to the parish documents. You should read Tate's *Parish Chest* (see Appendix 2) for wonderful accounts of documents originally stored in these chests.

The passing of the Parochial Records and Registers Measure of 1978 required all registers and other parish records over 100 years old to be deposited in appropriate archives, unless adequate controlled conditions of temperature and humidity for their safe storage could be provided by the parish. Only those registers still in use to record baptisms, marriages and burials may be kept in the parishes. All others may be consulted at county or similar record offices with other archives for that area. Most diocesan registries have now been closed and their archives, including the BTs, records of ordinations and appointments of parish officers, are deposited in county record offices, the county archivist acting as custodian of the diocesan records.

A considerable amount of material from Welsh parishes has been deposited in the National Library of Wales - which is a must for you to visit or contact if you have any Welsh ancestors. Scottish parish registers are likely to be in the GRO in New Register House; those for Ireland are in the Irish National Archives, although many of the registers which had been deposited in Dublin were destroyed in 1922. Parish registers for the Isle of Man are in either the Manx Library or the Register Office in Douglas, while those on Jersey are with either the incumbents or the Superintendent Registrar in the States Office. Guernsey, Herm and Jethou parish registers prior to 1840 are with the incumbents. On the Channel Islands it was customary for a married woman to include her maiden surname in many official and semi-official documents. Even some tombstones (see Chapter 8) show maiden surnames - so making your research a little easier.

Copies of registers

As well as the contemporary bishops' transcripts of parish registers, from the 19th Century the increasing awareness of historical documents caused a number of county record societies, antiquarian and even archaeological societies to transcribe and publish copies of parish registers. In some counties parish register societies were formed. The British Record Society and the Harleian Society were formed specifically to publish copies of certain archives. The Mormon (LDS) Church in the 20th Century microfilmed many parish registers of baptisms and marriages all over the world, including the British Isles. In Salt Lake City, USA, the films were transcribed and the entries fed into a computer to produce a county-by-county *Computer File Index (CFI)* which in 1979 was renamed the *International Genealogical Index (IGI)*. For the British Isles this index is very useful for locating baptisms and marriages in counties such as Lancashire or Kent where almost all of the registers are on film; but the *IGI* is of very little use in Northamptonshire, for example, where less than 3% of the registers have been filmed. Progressively more comprehensive editions of the *CFI/IGI* for the British Isles were published in 1973, 1975, 1976, 1978, 1980-81, 1984, 1988 and 1992. Copies of the microfiches are held in most county record offices and large reference libraries for their own and the surrounding counties. Many Family History Societies hold copies, and the Society of Genealogists and the Guildhall in London hold, in their libraries, microfiches of the *IGI* for the whole of the British Isles. The LDS Family History Centres around the world also have copies of these microfiches. The *IGI* is also available on CD-ROM which makes research, particularly when using the *Family Search* program, much easier at those Centres and libraries which have that facility. Extracts from the IGI are incorporated into the *Vital Records Index - British Isles*, available on CD-ROM, and continually being added to. You should be aware that the *IGI* also contains information submitted by individuals following their own research which may not have been very accurate. Accordingly you must use the *IGI* only as a finding aid to trace your British ancestors; names, dates and places should always be checked against the original records or microfilmed copies.

Do not forget that unlike civil registration of births and deaths, both original registers and BTs contain records of baptisms and burials, although occasionally dates of birth of those being baptised, and dates of death, and sometimes ages of those being buried, are also recorded. In most cases a child was baptised within a few days or weeks of being born, although there are some notable exceptions when a person was not baptised until just before being married. Occasionally a family of several brothers and sisters was baptised on the same day - perhaps because they had recently moved into a parish and in their former parish the incumbent was less interested. Or perhaps a new clergyman had been appointed to the parish and on visiting his new flock found a family whose parents had not been presenting their children for baptism as they went along. You will sometimes see a baptismal entry such as "Abraham, base son", or "natural son of Elizabeth Rose"; this indicates illegitimacy but occasionally you may find the name of the father (or the reputed father) alongside the baptismal entry. In Chapter 9 are some ideas on discovering the identity of fathers of illegitimate children.

From 1895 W P W Phillimore abstracted many entries from parish registers and published the results of his labours as books, now in large reference libraries. Percival Boyd spent many years in the 1930s studying mostly printed registers and marriage licences, abstracting marriage entries and compiling indexes of 7 million brides and grooms; the typescript copies of Boyd's work are in the library of the Society of Genealogists. The Pallot index of most marriages between 1780 and 1837 in the City of London is at the Institute of Heraldic and Genealogical Studies in Canterbury (see Appendix 1) who, for a fee, will search the index.

Other individuals and several county Family History Societies have transcribed and indexed marriages in their areas - the period 1813 to 1837 is particularly well covered. These transcriptions and indexes may help you to get back into the parish registers in the early 19th Century period from the census returns and immediately before the introduction of civil registration of births, marriages and deaths. You can check the availability of marriage indexes prepared by a Society or an individual in the relevant Gibson Guide (see Appendix 2); some are available on the Internet.

Migration

If you are very lucky, your ancestors were not adventurous, they stayed in the same parish for generations, and those parish registers back to the mid-16th Century have survived the ravages of time. In this case you may be able to trace your family to the beginning of the registers in 1538. However, this is unlikely as most people moved, if only a few miles, and many registers and even more BTs have been lost. But if you cannot find your ancestors in the anticipated parish records, try looking in those of the adjacent parishes. If they are not there either, try the next parish away, working radially outwards. A map of the area, showing roads, canals and railways is useful at this stage for you to see communication routes your ancestors may have used.

Depositions of court proceedings, especially of ecclesiastical courts, and education records are wonderful sources of the origins of migrants. Two Cameos in this series (see Appendix 2) detail these. A husband and wife often met for the first time at the local market or fair, so you should locate where these were held in relation to where you are looking for your ancestors. Try to put yourself in their shoes and imagine where they might have walked or ridden in search of work or a partner - remembering that our ancestors walked far further than we do today.

Where next?

Having exhausted parish registers and contemporary and modern abstracts and transcripts of them, banns books and marriage licence bonds and allegations, the next sources you can use in the hunt for information on your ancestors are wills and testaments, inventories and other probate records. The majority of these are freely available for you to study and we shall discuss these in Chapter 7. Church records of denominations outside the Established Anglican Church, and Anglican records, other than the registers we have just considered, may also have information on your ancestors. We shall discuss these in Chapter 8.

7. Probate Records

Wills, Testaments, Letters of Administration, Inventories

The relationships mentioned in a will, between a testator and other members of the family, will confirm the details you have found from civil registration, from census returns (or other lists of individuals), from parish registers or from BTs. If a parish register and the BT are missing you may be able to use a will to help piece your family tree together. The present whereabouts of wills and allied documents are identified later in this chapter. Sometimes individuals were not baptised when you anticipated - maybe not at all - and so even if the parish register or BT has survived, but your ancestors are not included, they may be mentioned in a will. A copy of a proved (probated) will may also have the date of death of the deceased noted at the end or on the back. Although the Statute of Wills formally legalised wills only from 1540, people were making wills in 1383 or even earlier - some Anglo-Saxon Wills have survived. Thus probate records may take you back into the 15th or earlier centuries, prior to the introduction of parish registers.

An ancestor's will, or a will witnessed by an ancestor, or a will in which your ancestor was a beneficiary or was appointed an executor (executrix, if a woman) by the testator, is always worthwhile trying to find. It may give you more than details on occupations and possessions, bed-linen, cutlery, crockery and kitchen utensils, crops, farming implements, livestock and investments or cash. A spouse, children, grandchildren, brothers, sisters, nieces and nephews, godchildren or friends may also be identified by name and sometimes with their ages, occupations and residences.

Strictly speaking, a will refers to real estate (land) and a testament to personalty (goods and chattels) - in fact the 1535 Statute of Wills made it illegal to dispose of land by testament; but often the term will is used to refer to either document. In Scotland a somewhat different distinction was made between heritable property (land and buildings) and moveable property (furniture, tools and animals). Normally the eldest son received all the heritable property on his father's death and so may not be mentioned in the will. A person making a will or a testament anywhere in the British Isles was termed a testator and all related documents (usually in Latin until 1733) were examined in a testamentary or probate court. A Testamentary Jurisdiction was territory over which a court claimed the right to grant probate.

Testators

Do not believe that only wealthy ancestors made wills but equally, just because an individual bequeathed large sums of money in a will did not mean there were sufficient assets to cover these. On occasions relatively poor persons left wills; after 1529 the courts granted probate free of charge if the deceased's effects were worth less than £5. (When a fee was charged many courts entered this into a Day Book.) Furthermore, your ancestors, while very much alive, may have split up their estates between friends and relations and so felt there was no need to make a will at all.

Until 1837 any boy over 14 and any girl over 12 could make a will; after that date a testator had to be over 21 for the will to be valid - although until 1882 a married woman had to get her husband's permission to make a will. Accordingly, if any of your female ancestors made a will before the 1882 Married Women's Property Act, you are likely to find that she was a spinster or a widow.

Generally a will was written out by a clerk or scrivener; but you may find a holograph will (hand-written by the testator) or even a nuncupative will - dictated in front of credible witnesses who later made sworn statements in the testamentary court. After 1837 nuncupative wills were acceptable only if made by military personnel or seamen on active service.

Probate before 1858

Before 1858 in England, Wales and Ireland (and before 1563 in Scotland) only the Ecclesiastical (Church) Courts, apart from some manorial and borough courts, could grant probate - prove wills and issue letters of administration; in other words they alone could authorize executors or administrators to carry out the terms of a will.

The British probate system was quite complicated but details of testamentary court procedures and exactly how individuals persuaded the appropriate church court to pass a Probate Act are simply, but very carefully, explained in the Cameo *Ecclesiastical Courts, Officials and Records: Sin, Sex & Probate* (see Appendix 2). However, you may find an outline of the procedures helpful here:

It was usual, if your ancestor's estate was in one or more parishes in one deanery or archdeaconry, for the will to be proved in the dean's or archdeacon's court, assuming that it had testamentary jurisdiction (some did not). If the estate was in two or more parishes in different archdeaconries, but in the same diocese, probate was granted in the bishop's court: if in two or more parishes in different dioceses but in the same province, probate was granted in an archbishop's prerogative court. A similar system (but without archdeacons' courts - see below) applied also to Ireland, the whole of which was in the province of Armagh with its own archbishop. If the estate was in the provinces of both Canterbury and York, or Canterbury and Armagh or York and Armagh, the Archbishop of Canterbury claimed superior jurisdiction and the will should have been proved in the Prerogative Court of Canterbury (PCC), although the Prerogative Court of York (PCY) handled some of these cases. The PCC proved wills of English and Welsh men and women who had property in England and Wales and who died at sea or otherwise out of the country (including Scotland). Families of the clergy and gentry occasionally took a will to a court higher than was strictly necessary, probably because they had greater confidence in the filing systems and administrative procedures of a higher court; probate of wealthy estates also tended to be handled in the higher courts.

As there were no archdeacons' courts in Ireland the 28 diocesan consistory courts or the Prerogative Court of Armagh (PCA) granted probate. The PCA proved wills for some Irish testators who had property in Ireland and other parts of the British Isles, although in some situations the PCC granted probate. Until 1816, when the Irish Testamentary Court was established in Henrietta Street, Dublin, probate in the PCA was granted at locations to suit the ecclesiastical judges. That material was subsequently, after the 1867 Public Records (Ireland) Act, transferred to the Irish Public Record Office - now the Irish National Archives, Dublin.

For the purposes of ecclesiastical administration, the Isle of Man was considered within the Province of York although the consistory and the archdeacon's courts on the Isle granted probate for most island residents from 1600 until 1885 when the High Court of Justice became responsible for probate. The Channel Islands after the Reformation were within the Diocese of Winchester in the Province of Canterbury; but probate on Jersey was granted by the Dean of Jersey from 1660 until 1949, and on Guernsey, Alderney, Sark, Herm and Jethou from 1660 to today by the Ecclesiastical Court of the Bailiwick of Guernsey.

Probate in Scotland

In Scotland from 1563, after the Reformation, probate was granted in one of 22 Commissary Courts until 31 December 1823, and after then in a Sheriff's Court. Commissariots (areas covered by the Commissary Courts) followed the same boundaries as the former Church Courts had used for their jurisdictions. Executors named in wills in Scotland had to be confirmed by a probate court - or if there was no will they were appointed and confirmed by the court. Thus the confirmations of executors are very useful probate records. You should look for a testament-testamentar if there was a will, a testament-dative if not. Probate was normally granted in the commissariot in which the testator died, but occasionally the Edinburgh commissary court granted probate for those who died anywhere in Scotland and for Scottish testators who died outside of Scotland. All commissariots' records to 1823 were indexed by the Scottish Record Society between 1897 and 1904 under the surnames of the deceased; women under their maiden surnames, cross-referenced from their husband's surnames. Copies of these index volumes are available in some large libraries.

Peculiar courts

Until 1858, rather than wills being proved in the court of either a dean, an archdeacon, a bishop (a commissary or consistory court), or an archbishop (a prerogative court), depending on the value and location of the property or where the deceased died, a peculiar court could be involved. A peculiar was a special or peculiar area covering one or more parishes or parts of a parish, in which the usual hierarchical ecclesiastical system of jurisdiction did not apply. You will find the records of the English and Welsh peculiar courts with the PCC material in the PRO or with the PCY material in the Borthwick Institute of Historical Research, University of York.

Probate and related documentation

Before 1700 it was customary for an itemized inventory to be made of a deceased's goods, but usually not of the real estate; this practice waned by about 1750 - although it should have been mandatory until 1783. Many inventories, indicating the value of each item, have survived and are filed with the probate material in appropriate archives. Details from inventories, often taken room by room in the home and out-houses, are extremely useful in reconstructing the life-styles of your ancestors.

You may discover, especially before 1858, that your forebears do not mention their land, held either by freehold or copyhold tenure, in their wills; this is because land traditionally descended to the next male in line (the heir-at-law) and so there was no need in such cases to refer to real estate in a will.

Do not worry unduly if your married ancestor does not refer to his wife in his will; it does not necessarily mean she had left him or died. When many couples were married, an indenture (an agreement, in this case a marriage settlement) was drawn up by which the wife was to be provided for in her widowhood.

Next of kin, or other interested parties, were granted Letters of Administration if the deceased was intestate (there was no will or no valid will) and they felt they had a claim on the property (real or personal) of the deceased.

Occasionally executors wouldn't (they renounced their rights) or couldn't (they were under age, or dead or could not be found) execute a will; in such a case an administrator was appointed, who signed an administration bond, to administer the estate - and Letters of Administration-With-Will-Annexed were granted by the Ecclesiastical Court. If an executor or administrator did not carry out the wishes of the testator - in other words failed to well and truly execute or administer probate - the interested parties could request the court to assign other persons (who signed assignation bonds or books) to do so.

Occasionally the beneficiaries, or those who believed they should have been beneficiaries, disputed the content of a will or the decision of a testamentary court. This could result in a Testamentary Suit - an appeal to a higher court. Although this might have been a nuisance at the time, this is good news for you if one of your ancestors was involved: details of a disputed probate case, if the arguments were protracted, may appear in an archdeacon's, a bishop's, and an archbishop's court and even in the High Court of Delegates until 1832 (the Judicial Committee of the Privy Council from 1833), or the Court of Arches (which acted as a court of appeal for both the PCC and the diocesan courts in the province of Canterbury). In these cases (known as Sentences in the PCC), the terms "By decree" or "Int Dec" (Interlocutory Decree) or "by Sent" are written into the documents. The court of appeal for the PCY was the Chancery Court of York or, in some cases until the late

17th Century, the York Consistory Court or, occasionally, the High Court of Delegates - see the Cameo *Ecclesiastical Courts, Officials and Records*.

From 1810 the Bank of England recognized probate that had been granted only by the PCC; thus if your ancestors were traders of any substance, their wills are probably in the PCC records irrespective of where they lived or died. A will was normally proved within a few weeks of the death of the testator - but occasionally because of a dispute or other complications, probate took considerably longer. I have been shown one case where probate was granted 75 years after the testator died. So do not give up if you cannot immediately find your ancestor's will - keep looking - it may be there somewhere!

Whereabouts of pre-1858 probate material
Probate records for the Prerogative Court of Canterbury are in the PRO, as are some surviving Anglo-Saxon wills. All have been indexed. The PCC material has been filmed and may be seen at the Family Records Centre or at Kew. The Prerogative Court of York material is in the Borthwick Institute, and the surviving Prerogative Court of Armagh material is in the Irish National Archives, although there are some pre-Reformation Irish wills at Trinity College, Dublin, at the Royal Irish Academy and in the English Public Record Office. All Scottish wills are in the National Archives of Scotland. Addresses of the above archives are in Appendix 1.

Originally the probate records of the deans', the archdeacons' and the bishops' courts were kept by diocesan registrars, but this material is now generally in deeds registries or the appropriate county archives. You may occasionally find a will, or a copy of one, among parish records in the county archives if the main beneficiary was "the parish". Much of the Welsh probate material is now in the National Library of Wales (see Appendix 1).

For a brief period during the Interregnum from 1653 to 1660 the Church Courts were closed and probate was granted by local Justices of the Peace. This documentation, which is in English, is held at the PRO. The manorial and borough courts, which had occasionally granted probate in some places, generally continued to operate during the Interregnum; their records are mostly in county archives.

From 1717 to 1791 estates of Roman Catholic (Papist) testators had to be registered (enrolled) in the Royal Courts at Westminster or with Justices of the Peace in County Courts prior to being proved in Church Courts. If you believe that your ancestors were Roman Catholics (professed the Popish Religion) during this era, you may find references to them in the E174, KB18 and FEC1 series at the PRO.

Associated with the ecclesiastical probate records are some Inland Revenue records resulting from a Stamp Duty being imposed on all probate granted from 1797 as a means of raising cash for fighting the Napoleonic Wars; these records, commonly called "Death Duty Registers", are in the IR series at the PRO. Indexes in microform are available at the Family Records Centre and at Kew.

Indexes or calendars to the testators of many probate records deposited both in county and in other archives have been prepared and published by organisations such the British Record Society, the Scottish Record Society and the Society of Genealogists.

Probate real estate records for Guernsey from 1841, when it became legally possible there to pass on land by will, are in the Greffe, St Peter Port; a comprehensive list of this material was published by the List and Index Society in 1969. Guernsey personalty records from 1660 are held by the ecclesiastical courts. Indexed probate real estate records for Jersey from 1851 (passing on real estate on Jersey became possible only in that year) are in the Greffe, St Helier. Indexed Jersey personalty wills from 1660 and calendared Letters of Administration from 1848 are also in the St Helier Greffe.

In Ireland from 1857, the bishops' Consistory Courts sent some, but by no means all, of their records to Dublin, to what is now the National Archives; there these were transcribed into books of wills, grants, and administration bonds which were indexed or calendared, some indexes being printed. In 1922, all but eleven of the original wills and letters of administration deposited in Dublin were destroyed, as were a few of the transcripts, although some Day Books and inventories and the majority of the indexes and calendars survived. To make up the loss of Irish probate records, since 1922 the authorities have been collecting copies of wills, some left in the bishops' consistory court archives and some held by solicitors; other copies have been discovered in private hands. This exercise is ongoing. The appendices to Reports of the Deputy Keeper of Public Records refer to the published works of Sir William Betham, T U Sadleir, W W Welply, W C Carrigan and others who had fortunately made abstracts from probate documents prior to their loss. Some probate material (some is copied) referring specifically to what is now Northern Ireland is in the Public Record Office of Northern Ireland (PRONI) in Belfast.

The county archivists throughout the British Isles can tell you what probate material they hold and what indexes are available to their own holdings. For some probate material, indexes of witnesses and beneficiaries are also available. A useful book, detailed county-by-county, is *Probate Records - Where to Look for Wills* by J S W Gibson (see Appendix 2).

Civil probate

On 12 January 1858 civil District Probate Registries were opened throughout England, Wales and Ireland, and the ecclesiastical probate courts closed. From then, probate has been granted and records kept by civil, not ecclesiastical, officials. Copies of the wills proved, and Letters of Administration granted, in English and Welsh civil courts have been sent to and kept by the Principal Probate Registry, now the Principal Registry of the Family Division at First Avenue House, London.

Very brief, but extremely useful abstracted information has been compiled into annual calendars or indexes, printed and arranged alphabetically under testators for both wills and Letters of Administration. These indexes have been filmed. The printed indexes for all of England and Wales are also available in some District Probate Registries, the National Library of Wales and some county record offices and reference libraries around the country. You can look at microfiche versions of the indexes to 1935 at the Family Records Centre. In these indexes you can discover the date probate was granted, the date and place of the testator's death and the residence of the deceased, the next of kin or beneficiaries and the value of the estate. For a fee you can see copies of the wills or Letters of Administration kept at First Avenue House and you may buy copies of these if you wish, although you can look through the indexes free of charge and make your own notes. If you want to order probate documents by post, you should write, **not** to First Avenue House, but to The Probate Registry, Postal Searches & Copies Department, Duncombe Place, York, YO1 2EA.

A similar system applies to the Irish probate material in Dublin and Belfast: copies of wills proved and letters of administration granted in the eleven Irish civil District Probate courts were kept by the Principal Probate Registry in Dublin from 1858, where indexes, similar to those at First Avenue House, were held in printed form. As in the case of pre-1858 probate material from the Ecclesiastical Courts, original civil probate records from 1858 held in Dublin were destroyed in 1922, although copies of the printed indexes, containing valuable data, have survived. From 1922 the copies of wills and administrations held in the District Probate Registries have been transferred to the National Archives in Dublin; or, in the case of the Armagh, Belfast and Londonderry District Probate Registries, to the Public Record Office in Belfast.

On the Isle of Man probate material can be researched in the Manx Museum Library. On Jersey the Ecclesiastical Courts continued to grant probate until 1948, although all probate material is housed at the Greffe, St Helier. Probate material for the other Channel Islands (apart from real estate on Guernsey) is still the responsibility of the ecclesiastical probate courts and is held by the Dean on Guernsey (see Appendix 1).

All Scottish probate records are in the National Archives of Scotland.

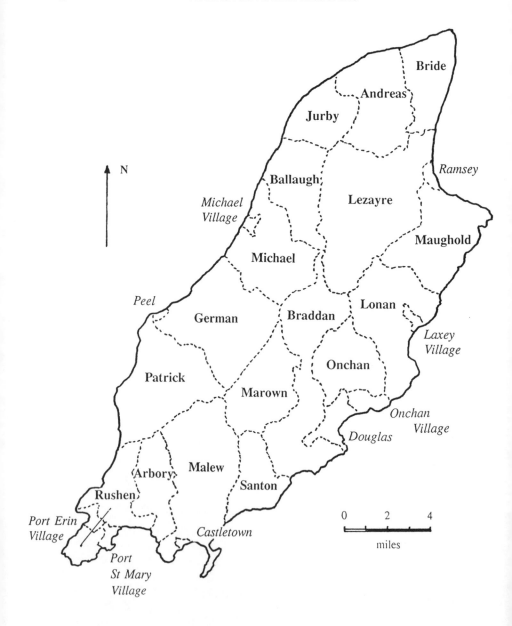

Isle of Man Towns, Village & Parish Districts

[Also see the maps on pages 20 and 24]

8. Other Church Records

Anglican, Nonconformist, Roman Catholic and Jewish

Besides expected ecclesiastical references, and parish registers and material relating to probate which we have discussed in Chapters 6 and 7, you can find, in the records of the Anglican Church, references to education (until today in some cases), to apprenticeship (by churchwardens or overseers to local or distant masters) to social security (although strictly the Poor Laws were administered by the secular authorities, but often within ecclesiastical boundaries until 1929), to emigration (assisted travel to other locations, even overseas), to professionals such as schoolmasters, surgeons, apothecaries and midwives (being granted licences to practise), and to aspects of maintaining law and order: cases of slander, sexual misbehaviour, non-payment of tithes and offences against church property were tried by the Ecclesiastical Courts.

As we discussed in Chapter 6, Henry VIII broke ties with the Pope in 1534 and declared himself Head of the Anglican Church. Soon after this time Papists loyal to the Roman Church were subjected to official persecution. From 1643 to 1660, strictly, the Established Church in Britain was Presbyterian (without an episcopacy; see below) rather than Anglican. Although the Protestants briefly lost control during the reign of Catholic James II, their influence was not lost and since 1688 the Established Anglican Church has remained Protestant with the reigning monarch as its titular head, and the Archbishop of Canterbury as its ecclesiastical head. After 1534 Roman Catholics thus became the initial dissenting Christian community that was separate from, and would not conform to, the Established faith throughout the British Isles.

The growth of dissent

There were other Christian groups, possibly including some of your ancestors, who chose to separate from and not conform to the practices of the Established Church, and would not consent to observe the Anglican faith; in some cases these Separatists, Dissenters or Nonconformists differed only slightly from the Anglican Church in their beliefs and practices, but in other cases their doctrines were totally polarised. Many such groups, even from the mid-16th Century, established their own congregations with churches, chapels, citadels and meeting houses in which to conduct their particular rites and services, often illegally and in the face of harsh opposition.

The Separatists were identified as a unique group in 1571, followed by Dissenters who first met on 20 November 1572 at Wandsworth, London; from these emerged Brownists in 1580, inspiring Congregationalists in 1592 who later became synonymous with Independents, although that term was not universally applied until 1640. Baptists were established in 1608, owing some of their origins to the Brownist Movement. The meeting of Dissenters in 1572 actually formed the first Presbytery in

England, but it was not until the formal abolition of the episcopacy (the recognition of archbishops and bishops as having ecclesiastical authority) by Parliament from 5 November 1643 that Presbyterianism was formally established. (You should note that when episcopacy was re-introduced with the Restoration of the Monarchy in 1660 many congregations followed Presbyterian doctrines.) The Arminians or Remonstrants who were founded in Holland in 1610, and may have influenced your continental European ancestors, were never firmly established in the British Isles. The term Nonconformist really applied in the British Isles to all the above groups from 24 August 1660 - the Act of Uniformity - but Dissenter and Nonconformist are used without any distinction by most authorities today.

The Society of Friends, often called Quakers (1646), Muggletonians (1651), Unitarians (1662), Glassites (1730 - evolving to Sandemanians in 1760), Calvinists (1735), Moravians (founded in 1736 but officially recognized in the British Isles in 1749), Inghamites (1753), Daleites or Old Independents (1770, mostly in Scotland - as were the McLeanists), Countess of Huntingdon's Connexion (1779), Swedenborgians, also known as the New Church or New Jerusalem Church (in England established in 1783), Methodists (1784) - who soon split into the Methodist New Connexion (1797), Primitive Methodists (1812), Bible Christians (1815), and Protestant Methodists (1828), some of whom came together as the United Methodist Free Church (1857) and others re-joined in 1932, leaving the Methodist Reform Union and the Independent Methodist Church to this day, Universalists (1792), Southcottians (1800), Darbyites (1827) who became Plymouth Brethren, Irvingites, also known as the Catholic Apostolic Church (1832), Campbellites (founded in America in 1827, the first Church being opened in England in 1836), the Church of Jesus Christ of Latter-day Saints (also founded in America but in 1830, the first missionaries arriving in England in 1837), Christadelphians or Thomasites (1848), Salvation Army (1865), International Bible Students (1872, who became Jehovah's Witnesses in 1931) and Church of Christ, Scientist (1879) are examples of denominations that built separate churches and most of which maintained their own records.

Additionally, certain Protestant communities suffering persecution in Continental Europe sought refuge and established their own Churches in the British Isles from the 16th Century with their own series of records. Examples of these are the Dutch and French Walloon and Huguenot congregations. The Jewish communities built synagogues and kept records of their services and ceremonies from the middle of the 17th Century.

Very many of the records of the Churches referred to in this section were surrendered in 1840 to the Registrar General; these are now in the RG4 and RG6 series at the PRO, London. This material has been microfilmed. As many of these films have been bought by libraries around the world, you may be able to study these records without travelling to London.

Monastic records

The Christian Church in the British Isles before the Reformation, as we discussed above, was tied to the Church of Rome; many ecclesiastical and secular facilities and opportunities were provided in monasteries. Although these religious houses were largely dissolved by Henry VIII from 1536, a not insignificant number of their records such as *Chartularies, Registers, Obituaries, Calendars* and *Chronicles* survived. Many are now preserved in the British Library, the PRO and in the University Libraries at Oxford and Cambridge. Monastic records contain biographical and genealogical information and details which you will find of interest if you have got back to before the beginning of parish registers in 1538. Many of these archives were transcribed, translated from Saxon and Latin and published by antiquarian and county historical and record societies from the middle of the 19th Century. This scholarly activity continues so that today you can have the luxury of reading ancient records in a convenient form.

Chartularies contain copies of charters relating to property of religious houses, at least one containing a history of the founder's family. *Leiger* and *Cowcher Books* were less-formally compiled Chartularies. *Registers* contain names of members and patrons of religious houses and in many cases their genealogies. The revenues and possessions and names of occupants of property belonging to the monastery were also entered in the registers. Some marriages and burials were recorded, thus pre-dating parish registers. *Obituaries*, also termed *Necrologies*, recorded deaths and biographical details on benefactors, monarchs and Church officials such as archbishops, bishops, abbots, priests and monks. *Calendars* and *Martyrologies* were almanacs indicating the days on which to commemorate a particular birthday or anniversary of death or benefaction. *Chronicles* were diaries or recordings of note-worthy topical events taking place on monastic property or relating to a local family.

Additional monastic records contain lists of names of notable individuals (could one have been an ancestor of yours?) who attended particular events or festivals; the Battle Abbey Roll, Crusade Rolls and Henry VIII's Tournament Roll are typical.

Records of the Anglican Church

Prior to the break from Rome, *Confirmation* or the imposition or laying-on of hands was regarded as a sacrament, as was baptism and the eucharist. Subsequently, however, it became a confirmation by our individual ancestors of baptismal vows formerly taken on their behalf by their godparents or sponsors. From 1661 the Book of Common Prayer provided a form of words to express this confirmation. Some churches kept separate records of those who were confirmed; for others the only evidence you will be able to find that a confirmation was held at all at the church is in the diocesan records, as a bishop normally conducted the service.

Churchwardens' accounts refer to activities such as collecting *pew rents* from your ancestors, which may attach details of where they sat in the church (*seating plans*) and repairs to the fabric of the church which often show names of craftsmen undertaking the work. There were other records of income and expenditure handled by the churchwardens, associated with individuals and the parish church; examples are those created by levying and collecting *Church rates*, aspects of looking after the disadvantaged of the parish, the poor and parish apprentices, possibly by assisting them to emigrate to potentially brighter opportunities elsewhere, often in collaboration with the overseers. These may provide the vital clue you are seeking when some of your ancestors are "missing" from the parish where you were expecting to locate them. Today all these records are in county or similar archives.

Terriers are lists of Church possessions drawn up and submitted to the appropriate archdeacon or bishop as a result of an instruction of 1571. These are, accordingly, now in diocesan archives which may be in county record offices. The lands or *glebes* from which tithes may also have been derived, as well as property, livestock and implements belonging to the local churches, appear on these terriers. You will find these from 1600 to 1820 particularly useful in providing details on your British ancestors. *Tithe Maps* and *Apportionments* (see Chapter 10) contain many names of tenants and landlords.

Vestry minutes are the record of discussions and decisions made at meetings of the Vestry or the Select Vestry - the local community or its representatives assembling to deliberate its business and affairs. At these meetings the churchwardens' accounts and those of other church officials were reviewed, and the views of local decision-makers were aired. The Vestry met either in the Church itself, or in a room over the Church porch, or sometimes in the local alehouse or inn. You can discern from the state of the writing of the minutes which meetings were held where!

Licences granted to surgeons and schoolmasters, mentioned above, were granted by the Archdeacons' Ecclesiastical Courts, held possibly every six weeks. At these courts cases of improper conduct were also heard; as they made up so much of court business they became known as "Bawdy Courts". Even non-attendance at Church services, perhaps by one of your ancestors, was punished from 1562 by these courts imposing amercements (financial penalties) of one shilling per service missed; in 1592 this penalty was increased to twenty shillings a month. After 1641 the Church Courts could no longer impose amercements. These records may be found in county archives. The activities of other Ecclesiastical Courts, such as Consistory Courts, Courts of Audience, Convocation Courts, Chancery Courts, the Court of High Commission and their records and those of Doctors' Commons, the ecclesiastical legal academy, are described in the Cameo on Ecclesiastical Courts quoted above.

Bishops' Licences were granted, at the equivalent of an ecclesiastical court sitting, for a variety of causes: to a curate to officiate or to a minister to expound; to an incumbent to reside elsewhere than on his benefice; to hold benefices in plurality; to engage in trade, to occupy a farm greater than eighty acres (except on his own glebe); to appoint fasts; to exorcise devils; to a layman to eat flesh or to marry in Lent. Faculties were issued by a bishop permitting or enabling the local church authorities to alter the fabric of their church, to erect a monument, to obtain additional ornaments or utensils, to reserve a vault, or to build on church land. The documentation associated with a faculty was filed in the diocesan archives.

As the literacy of parishioners improved during the 19th Century, weekly or monthly Church Magazines or Parish Newsletters were published. These often contain biographical notes on local individuals as well as details on past and future events in the parish, rural deanery, archdeaconry, diocese or province. Back issues are not so easily found, but if the county archives do not have copies you may be lucky to discover them in a local history library or even with the present incumbent.

Whilst not strictly church records, the Poor Law settlement and removal certificates (see Chapter 9) from the 1600s to the 1800s were often kept in the Parish Chest with Church documents; these are now located with parochial material in county record or similar offices, as are the associated Poor Law accounts and the Poor Rate Books.

A separate category of Church records associated with the Anglican Church does not belong to a specific parish and so the records are termed non-parochial. Some of these non-parochial Church records are in county archives, some have been deposited in the PRO while others are still retained by the body concerned. Examples of such records are the registers of Fleet (and other clandestine) marriages, of institutional and school chapels, of cathedrals and collegiate churches, of the Chapels Royal and of workhouse and proprietary chapels - such as those attached to the Inns of Court and to the Royal Hospital in Chelsea.

Records of Roman Catholics

As the Roman Catholic Church was not officially recognized in the British Isles after 1534 for many years, and furthermore many Catholics suffered severe persecution, they maintained no registers initially. In fact, Recusants' Rolls were drawn up annually from 1562 as lists of non-attenders at services of the Established Church; whilst mostly of Roman Catholics, denominations of individuals were not stated. These rolls compiled for each county bear names, family relationships, places of residence, status, occupations, amercements paid and dates between which they applied. The rolls are in the PRO [E376 & 377 series] but there are some local lists of non-attenders. Lists specifically of Papists were compiled in 1680, 1705/6, 1767 and 1781, although the first Catholic Relief Act came into force in 1778.

Catholics' estates had to be registered with Clerks of the Peace from 1717 to 1791 prior to probate being granted. Gradually religious toleration enabled communities to be re-established, to build their own chapels and churches and to record their own activities (although legally they were not permitted their own places of worship until 1832). Acts of Parliament granting official toleration hastened this process, particularly after 1791. Marriages were not legally recognized if conducted in a Roman Catholic Church until 1837 (even later in most instances - see the Cameo on Marriage) although several Catholic registers include marriages.

Some Catholic Church registers, particularly from Yorkshire, were surrendered to the Registrar General in 1840 and 1858, others have been deposited in county archives, but many are still held by local Churches. A few have been transcribed and published by the Catholic Record Society (see Appendix 1), copies of whose volumes you can consult in most large reference libraries. The *Catholic Directory* from 1837 gives details of present-day Catholic dioceses, clergy and organisations.

Records of Nonconformists

Similarly to the Roman Catholic communities, other dissenting congregations were often subject to persecution - and to avoid detection did not initially maintain registers. The records of activities obviously reflect their particular faiths; the Baptists, for example, believing in the baptism solely of believers, which normally meant adults, did not have infant baptismal registers although there may be records of children being dedicated. The Southcottians practised, though not very skilfully on occasions, circumcision. There appear to be no Nonconformist registers in the British Isles before 1641.

The Society of Friends was among the first to establish records; digests (abstracts of essential information) of their registers are at the Friends House Library in London (see Appendix 1). In fact Quaker marriage registers were kept so meticulously, as were those of the Jews, that they were awarded the same status as those of the Established Anglican Church: in other words marriages performed according to their own rites for their own members and registered by Quaker and Jewish congregations were accepted as valid, unlike those for other Dissenters or Nonconformists - who, until 1837, had to attend an Anglican marriage ceremony if their marriage was to be valid and their children, thereby, legitimate. There are many Presbyterian and Independent Church records commencing between 1662 and 1700; these denominations joined with the Baptists in 1743 to centralise their birth registrations at Dr Williams's Library. This collection of 50,000 entries to 1837 is in the PRO [RG 4 & 5 series] and indexed in the Mormon *Vital Records Index - British Isles.*

Most Nonconformist registers were surrendered to the Registrar General in 1840 and 1858; these may also be consulted at the PRO, although they have been microfilmed and so are available elsewhere as well. Since 1858 many registers and records of the Dissenting Churches have been lodged in denominational depositories (see Appendix 1), county record offices or local libraries although some are retained by the Church locally. A few have been transcribed and published.

In contrast, registers of foreign Protestant Churches in England, such as those of Huguenot and Walloon congregations, have been indexed and published by the Huguenot Society of London. Most Nonconformists publish their own denominational handbooks and yearbooks containing information on their Churches and ministers. Denominational magazines and journals, similar to Parish Newsletters of the Established Church, are useful records from the nineteenth century onwards.

Many Nonconformist congregations also kept Church Membership Rolls and Minutes' Books of their business meetings.

Records of Jews

Although Jews were expelled from England in 1290, they were permitted to settle from the mid-17th Century, and within fifty years the first Synagogue was built in London. Jewish records commence from this time; because Jews were permitted to conduct marriages according to their own rites, their registers of the Ketubah (marriage contract) are important, particularly after 1754. Birth Registers commence later. Some Circumcision Registers were maintained by individual mohels (operators), rather than associated with particular synagogues, in which cases they refer to a variety of locations.

Most Jewish records and registers are retained by local synagogues although several in London have been collected centrally (see Appendix 1). It is useful if you can read the entries in Hebrew in the records, or find someone to do this for you, rather than the English versions or translations, as a more comprehensive family relationship is often apparent in the original Hebrew.

Church schools

Most Churches in the British Isles, whether of the Established faith, of the Roman Catholic faith, of most Nonconformists, or Jewish Synagogues, had associated schools or other educational academies or institutions. The records of these Church Schools, stretching from the earliest archives to the present with biographical details on teachers and pupils, are fully described in the Cameo on Education (see Appendix 2).

Monumental inscriptions

Although not normally considered as Church records, inscriptions to the dead on monuments, memorials, effigies, brasses, graves, tombstones, and church furniture and ornaments often record information not available elsewhere. Burial or death registers rarely contain more than names and not always ages of the deceased. In contrast a memorial often bears an occupation, date of birth, relationship to others and sometimes additional biographical information.

Almost all denominations of the Churches and Jewish communities in the British Isles have their own burial grounds or use private or public cemeteries where you can spend many happy hours deciphering inscriptions. Several were transcribed many years ago, others more recently, and some have been indexed, copies of which you can consult in local archives or in national collections such as that held by the Society of Genealogists.

You should be aware, however, that some 19th Century researchers were quite selective in the memorials they chose to examine. Accordingly, a number of transcribed lists of a particular graveyard or burial ground are incomplete, perhaps having only the names of the local gentry or of the extended family in which the transcriber was interested. Conversely, some details copied in the past are indecipherable today, so do look at old and newer lists of monumental inscriptions.

Wooden funeral hatchments, associated with armigerous families (see Chapter 13), which were paraded in funeral processions, sometimes found their way to parish churches, and are displayed there to this day. Similar Church records are wooden benefactors' boards, also in churches throughout the British Isles; these indicate sums of money or amounts of bread to be distributed to the poor from a gift or endowment by an individual who may also have formally established a Charity to be administered by the local Church authorities.

9. Old and New Poor Laws
Social Security Records from 1285 to 1966

Social security in the British Isles is not a novel product of the 20th Century even if the legislation and statutes in England of 1966 and earlier in 1948 were milestones in its history; and in 1929 the responsibilities of local guardians to administer the Poor Laws were transferred to county authorities and subsequently taken over by central government. Nor were the Poor Laws conjured out of thin air in 1597 as some books on this topic would have you believe; the origins of poor relief in the British Isles are with the arrival of Christianity a thousand years before.

Over the centuries successive monarchs and governments at national and local levels attempted to solve the interwoven problems of poverty and law and order through the enactment of multitudinous Poor Laws. The records compiled in the administration of those laws are brimming over with names and descriptions of your ancestors, all of whom were exposed to these problems. From the 16th to the 20th Centuries such problems were wrestled with on a local basis, initially at county division (such as a hundred) level, then parochial and then back at county level, as the parish became too small a unit to meet the varied needs of the impoverished. In this chapter we shall summarize some of the legislation to enable you to appreciate its effects. A far more comprehensive account of the Poor Laws can be found in the Cameo *They Removed My Poor Ancestors* (see Appendix 2).

Records which are of particular use to you fall into two distinct series: those of the "Old Poor Laws" before 1834 (1838 in Ireland and 1845 in Scotland), and those of the "New Poor Laws" from 1834 (1838 and 1845) to 1929. Under the "Old Poor Laws" the systems were more or less parochially administered; under the "New Poor Laws" Boards of Guardians of the Poor, within areas termed Unions, were responsible for caring for the unemployed. Records from 1929, when the system was administered by a central government department specifically set up for the purpose, are not readily available for public research.

It is possible, by consulting the records that have survived, from both the national intentions to alleviate unemployment, and the county interpretation of the legislation, and then the local execution or enactment of the Poor Laws, for you to glean a vivid picture of your ancestors - whether they were those who received relief or possibly those who contributed cash or kind towards its payment; or perhaps those who acted as overseers in its distribution or as constables or justices in its administration.

13th to 16th Centuries
The 1285 Statute of Winchester required strangers in a parish to be arrested after sunset and legislation in 1331 confirmed that all "nightwalkers" should be arrested. Donations to the jobless who were capable of work were forbidden in 1349, while in 1383 judges, justices and sheriffs were given power "to enquire of all vagabonds and

feitors and their offences, to examine them and compel them to find surety or otherwise go to gaol until the next quarter sessions". The records of judges, justices and sheriffs and the courts over which they presided at assizes, quarter and petty sessions and tourns respectively, form yet another rich source of information for the following 600 years which you could use in tracing your British ancestors. These courts dealt with all aspects of maintaining law and order, with licences to enable people to better adhere to statutes and local by-laws, and sentenced those who committed crimes or felonies or otherwise failed to keep the peace. Most assize and some sheriffs' records are in national collections - the PRO, for example. In general, other records of sheriffs and those of the justices are in county and regional archives. If any of your British ancestors were convicts (transported to America, Gibraltar, Bermuda or Australia), or indentured servants (transported to America), or other criminals or felons, you will find these records extremely interesting.

In 1388 all artificers, labourers, servants and victuallers, and even pilgrims, were prohibited from departing from their homes without the written permission of a Justice of the Peace - and this permission had to be carried at all times. An ancestor of yours found wandering without a testimonial letter would have been regarded as a vagrant and put in the stocks. Thus the necessary letter became known as a "Vagrant's Pass". Under the 1388 Statute all beggars impotent to serve (incapable of work) were ordered to remain where they were when the Act was passed. Any who couldn't be maintained locally were returned to their birthplaces. The principle of unemployed persons being sent or taken back, "removed", to their places of origin was, therefore, put into place in the 14th Century.

An Act of 1495 "Against Vagabonds and Beggars", and another in 1504, moderated the provisions of the 1383 Act and compelled beggars incapable of work to return home. An important distinction was emerging between those who couldn't work and those who wouldn't.

The impotent (disabled) jobless were enabled from 1530 to register with local Justices of the Peace for permission to beg within authorized limits. Impotent beggars without licences were to be stripped to the waist and whipped or put in the stocks and then given a licence. Other "idle persons", such as fortune-tellers, were to be whipped for two days; for their second offence were to be scourged for two days, then put in the pillory for two hours and to have one ear cut off; for a third offence to suffer similar punishment with whipping and standing in the pillory and to have the other ear cut off. Every beggar "whole and mighty in body and able to labour" (the able-bodied unemployed) was to be "tied to the end of a cart naked and beaten with whips throughout the town till his body be bloody", sworn to return home and then to "put himself to labour like as a true man ought to do". The distinction was reinforced between those who couldn't work and those who wouldn't.

Further Acts in 1535, 1547, 1549, 1551, 1562 and 1572 encouraged parishes to collect alms and provide support for the disabled unemployed and work for those capable of work (the sturdy beggars) who were being returned home. The punishments for non-compliance continued to be harsh with one or both ears being cut off or mutilated, and persistent offenders being branded with a V or S, using a hot iron. Being confined to the stocks or pillory for one, two or three days, being whipped and being fed only bread and water, or being chained around the neck or leg were methods also available for Justices to punish offenders. As government policies changed, begging licences were introduced, withdrawn and reintroduced with the additional requirement from 1562 for your poor ancestor to wear a "notable badge or token on the breast and back of his outermost garment". Parish Alms Collectors and Distributors had been introduced in 1551, but in 1572 a totally new post, that of Overseer of the Poor, was created to look after pauper relief.

From 1575 Houses of Correction were to be provided in every county. The mothers and reputed fathers of illegitimate children, causing some of the parish funds to be spent on their "bastards begotten and born out of wedlock", were to pay for the upkeep of their children - or go to gaol awaiting trial at the next quarter sessions. Further Acts were introduced in 1589 and 1593 to minimize problems created by the homeless poor. The value to you of this legislation is that most offenders were taken to the local civil courts, Petty Sessions, Quarter Sessions, or sometimes dealt with at a Manorial Court - and many of these court records are now in county archives. Some material has been indexed under surnames, which makes your searching for an ancestor much easier. Fathers (or reputed fathers) of illegitimate children, as we mentioned in Chapter 6, can sometimes be found in this class of record.

Many articles on the Poor Laws give the impression that the relevant legislation commenced only in 1597 and that overseers were appointed then for the first time. Having read the above paragraphs, obviously you do not believe this. Nevertheless, 1597 remains a significant year as a compulsory rate was introduced then to finance unemployment assistance (poor relief) to be administered by churchwardens and two to four of the new overseers selected annually by the Vestry or the Manorial Court. You will find in general that the records of these overseers are superb for the following three centuries. The 1597 Act made provision to set the able-bodied jobless to work and provide for the old (those over 50), the physically and mentally sick and the disabled who could not support themselves.

17th to 19th Centuries
In 1601 a temporary Act was introduced to reinforce and revise the 1597 Act. Every parish was to be responsible for relieving its own jobless by cash payment or in the form of housing, rent relief, repairs to buildings or gifts of fuel. By the 1700s, as more doctors and medicine became available, medical bills were paid for; infirmaries were introduced in the 1750s. From the inception of relief in 1601, money to pay for this was raised by taxing all occupiers of property within the parish, according to "their ability to pay" (their income). This scheme failed miserably and a system based on the rentable value of property was introduced. In 1601 the concept of out-

door relief only had been conceived; in-door relief (the workhouse) was not forthcoming for a hundred years.

The temporary 1601 Act was prolonged in 1603 and again in 1627, becoming permanent in 1640. However, in 1609 it was noted that Houses of Correction proposed in 1575 were not being built, so an Act in that year restated the intentions. Where there were no Houses of Correction the justices themselves were each fined. In addition constables were to search out rogues in each parish, apprehend vagrants, and take them before magistrates for committal to the Houses of Correction. "Lewd women with bastards" and parents who abandoned their children were also to be committed.

In 1662 the (so-called) First Act of Settlement legalised removal of potentially chargeable immigrants. This concept was not new, as you saw above in the 1388 legislation, but removal now had to take place within forty days of arrival. Exemptions were: (a) persons who rented a tenement for £10 or more per year, (b) those who, if they became chargeable, could give the parish security for its indemnity, (c) those who travelled for temporary or seasonal work and who had a certificate from their own parish officers agreeing to take them back. The Act also enabled justices to order the transportation to the plantations (America) of incorrigible rogues, vagabonds and sturdy beggars. Perhaps one of your ancestors enjoyed the enactment of this legislation! Within exceptionally large parishes each township was to care for its unemployed; but these provisions created some administrative confusion, especially in towns, causing a number of Local Acts to be introduced, particularly from 1696 to solve the problems. Some felt that the 1662 legislation was too sympathetic towards the immigrant and over the next few years further Acts were introduced to redress the inequality.

In 1685 and 1691 the conditions for legalised removal were modified and notice of any removal was read out in the parish church and entered in the overseers' account book. If one of these has survived for "your" parish, you may find your ancestors mentioned. Whilst this did tilt the balance against the immigrant there were additions to the list of circumstances for gaining settlement without having to give written notice: (a) serving for one year as a parish officer, if unmarried, (b) paying the parish rate, (c) being bound apprentice to a master living within the parish; all of these created yet more sources where you can seek your ancestors.

In 1696 a local Act of Parliament was introduced in Bristol to resolve the problems of the previous 100 years requiring local interpretation of national legislation. A workhouse was involved in this scheme thereby introducing the concept of in-door relief. Other towns, especially in the west of England, soon followed suit with similar local Acts; there is a list of those in Eden's *State of the Poor*, published in 1797. References to relevant other and post-1797 Acts are given in the Cameo *They Removed My Poor Ancestors*. If you want to read the Acts themselves, you will have to visit a specialist law library, although the pertinent county record offices should have copies of their local Acts of Parliament.

From 1697 Parish Pension lists were to be drawn up and settlement could be gained also by unmarried persons hired for a year as servants; so you will find many employers taking on staff for only 364 days at a time. The unemployed (poor, as they were called then) had to wear cloth badges displaying the letter P and the initial letter of their parish. The law regarding certificates was also extended to cover permanent movements; but to be valid, certificates had to be issued by overseers and churchwardens, attested by two witnesses and approved by two justices. Very many certificates, particularly until the reforms of 1795, have survived. Removal orders and examination papers have also survived. Try looking for certificates relating to your ancestors among the parish documents and quarter sessions records.

A Workhouse-test Act was introduced in 1722 whereby those who refused to move into a workhouse could be denied relief. Powers to establish workhouses were made available to all parishes. The concept of Parish Unions was introduced; but as parishes could select their own partners and could leave one Union and join another at a whim, chaos ensued for the next sixty years.

The question of payment for removal from one parish to another was resolved in 1729, that this should be borne by the parish of settlement. Three years later, because reputed fathers of bastards were not paying for their responsibilities, any person charged on oath with being the father of a bastard child could be committed to gaol. So gaol lists, as well as the quarter sessions records, are worth seeking out.

From 1743 vagrants who were apprehended were to be whipped or confined and then removed to their place of settlement. Vagrants were classified as either "idle and disorderly", or "rogues and vagabonds", or "incorrigible rogues". Those who returned to the parish from which they had been removed, or who had begged in their own parish, or who had even only threatened to leave their dependents, were to be regarded as idle and disorderly. Those who actually left their dependents were regarded as rogues and vagabonds, as were any found wandering around, deceiving, begging, or unlawfully trading. Incorrigible rogues included those who had previously committed an offence as a rogue or a vagabond, or those who had escaped from custody or a House of Correction while being considered a rogue, or those who refused to be examined or those who gave false evidence at their examination by the justices when settlement or removal was being investigated. Bastard children of vagrant women were not to gain settlement necessarily in the parish of their birth but in the parish of their mother's legal settlement. Incorrigible rogues were to be imprisoned for six months, whipped at the justices' discretion, and either removed to their parish of settlement, or impressed into military service with the army or navy (see Chapter 11). In the same year a later Act required overseers to keep "proper" poor accounts.

The collection of money to finance relief, introduced by the Church in 1690, was formally authorized by Parliament in 1748. (The accounts, with names of contributors, were not printed until 1821 when they were published in Parliamentary Papers IV.) In 1775, and almost annually from then, Select Committees were appointed to investigate various aspects of unemployment relief and vagrancy.

Gilbert's Act (sometimes referred to as a Workhouse Act even though the concept was sixty years old) was introduced in 1782 to reinforce the idea of parish Poor Law Unions. In 1792, as apprenticeships for the jobless were being abused in some parts of the country, the whole system was brought under closer control. Fortunately, some of these parish apprenticeship documents have survived for you to see.

In 1795 the inconsistent practices regarding settlement were generalized by statute: all jobless persons were to be given the status of certificatemen, as nobody should have been removed until actually a charge on a parish; and those unfit to travel were not to be forcibly removed. In the meantime the parish of settlement was to pay the relief which had been awarded by the parish of residence. Later on in 1795 the 1722 and 1782 Workhouse Acts were amended to enable justices to grant out-door relief in cases of temporary need.

From this time the volume of paperwork, and so of the surviving records available to you today, increased: orders of supervision if the jobless were too sick to travel, papers dealing with financial arrangements between parishes, and bulky correspondence. Even before 1795 it was realised that transmitting paper and money was preferable to transferring people, but the Act added impetus to the documentation.

By 1802 the practice had grown up of sending young children, particularly from the rural south, to the new textile mills in the expanding industrial north of England, where they were exposed to little supervision or protection. To provide some safeguards an Act was introduced requiring a register to be kept in each parish of the binding by overseers of apprentices to masters - especially where the two parties were from distantly separated parishes.

The realisation that mentally disordered persons required particular care (though we wouldn't today necessarily agree on the treatment offered) caused an Act to be introduced in 1808 to deal with jobless lunatics. This Act required lunatic asylums offering treatment and accommodation to be provided on a county basis. Wearing badges by the unemployed had not in general been enforced during the latter part of the 18th Century; recognizing this in 1810, the Parliament of the day withdrew this compulsion. In 1816 the binding of apprentices to masters in distant parishes was still of some concern; accordingly a Parliamentary Act endorsed and improved the terms of the 1802 Act and insisted that justices approved all such apprenticeships.

Elected Overseers of the Poor had officially been unpaid since 1597, although there was provision that an elected individual need not take up the post if he paid a deputy to take his place. In 1819, under the Sturges Bourne Act, parishes were given the power to hire paid Assistant Overseers. In fact, there were some parishes and Unions supporting a workhouse who had appointed a Governor who was already by custom (unlawfully before this Act) paid. This Act also provided the framework for Select Vestries to be elected by the parish ratepayers at a Vestry Meeting; overseers could then consult the Select Vestry without waiting for an annual Vestry Meeting.

The New Poor Law

The above national and local Poor Law Acts (we have outlined only a selection here), did much to bridle corrupt practices. But it was not until 1834 that a thorough review of the entire system culminated in a Royal Commission producing a major report. The Poor Law Amendment Act of 1834 introduced a major change in the administrative arrangements for dealing with assistance for the unemployed. The former concept of each parish caring for its jobless was replaced by the 1722 idea that groups of parishes should take responsibility for an area, termed a Union (as those parishes were encouraged to unite or be "in union", with a common aim to provide for their impoverished). In each Union the impotent poor (disabled jobless) were accommodated in a workhouse and Boards of Guardians of the Poor were appointed to administer the new system of in-door and out-door welfare. In many cases a Union was given the same name as the place where the workhouse stood. It was still several years before the recommendations of the report were carried out in some areas. The Guardians administered the "New Poor Law" until 1929.

Poor Law Records

Whilst the pre-1834 records do not survive for every part of every county, you will discover that some are readily available, having been printed in calendar, abstract or other form. The way in which the quarter sessions records were kept varies from county to county, although in general there are: the main record of the court - an Order or Minute Book (or both); bundles of administrative papers to support the main record; various documents deposited or registered at the court. The post-1834 Guardians' records, in general, have survived well and in most county and similar archives are kept separately from parish documents. Many Guardians' records contain names and ages of heads of households and the relief given; on occasions the compilers included addresses, non-relief incomes, notes on disabilities, reasons for needing relief and similar information on dependents - in fact mini family histories.

Correspondence between the Poor Law Commission in London (until 1847 and the Poor Law Board after then) and county Guardians was voluminous; it often referred to individuals by name as well as conditions in the Unions, menus for workhouse meals and so on. You can read all this in the Public Record Office [MH series]; over 16,000 volumes of correspondence are in MH12 alone. Correspondence from 1900 is in MH68, although some was destroyed in World War II. You will find information on pauper emigration in MH19/22 and the appointment of officers in each Union from 1837 to 1921 in MH9 and MH19. Schooling of the poor from 1848 to 1910 is in MH 27. Gibson's *Poor Law Union Records* (see Appendix 2) details 1834-1930 material.

Many people, including children, died whilst in workhouses, others were born there. Hence you may find some useful information in their registers, now in county and similar archives. In addition there are county enclosure, tithe, and other maps (see Chapter 10) which can give the location of workhouse buildings; county land tax returns give a record of parish officers; and there are Boards of Guardians' Minutes and Accounts, workhouse registers and punishment books.

The unemployed in Scotland

In Scotland the care of the unemployed, as in England, was assumed by Church and Crown until the Reformation. In 1579 and 1661 Scottish Parliamentary Acts, similar to the 1572, 1597 and 1601 English Acts, made heritors (landowners) and the kirk session in each parish responsible for their jobless. A major difference in Scotland was the lack of use of compulsory giving to a poor rate, reliance being placed on voluntary contributions; furthermore, no relief was available for the able-bodied unemployed and there was little provision for workhouses. As a result the 1845 Poor Law Amendment Act in Scotland (similar to the 1834 English Act) established "poor-houses" and compulsory assessment for contributions. Parochial Boards, similar to the Boards of Guardians in England and Wales, were set up to administer relief. In 1894 the Parochial Boards were replaced by parish councils; and hence it is in their records that you should look for references to your jobless (poor) Scottish ancestors. The Sheriffs' Courts also dealt with many cases of applications for relief. All this material is in the National Archives of Scotland in Edinburgh.

The unemployed in Ireland

In Ireland there was no direct relief for the jobless until the 1838 Irish Poor Law Act, following the first Report on the Poor in 1836. This initially expressly prohibited out-door relief, concentrating on provision within workhouses, hospitals, institutions and district schools. But because of the disastrous potato famine, an 1847 Extension Act made out-door relief available. Surviving records are in the Irish National Archives.

Charities

You should remember that across the whole of the British Isles, privately and publicly supported charities and children's societies (see Pauline Saul's *Enquire Within* and the Cameo *They Removed my Poor Ancestors*) also played a major role in alleviating poverty. The Foundling Hospital from 1745 and the British Lying-In Hospital from 1749 welcomed the distressed poor; whilst both were in London, many of their "customers" came from elsewhere. Foundling hospitals were opened in other places in the British Isles from the late 1850s. You should consult the records of these charitable institutions and the hospitals and infirmaries they supported, many of which are in county and regional archives. But several organisations, still operating today, have their own records where you may find information on your ancestors. The *Charities Digest* (see Appendix 2), published annually since 1882 for the Family Welfare Association, has details on such organisations; look particularly under Children's Welfare, Education and Orphans.

10. Land Records

The Owners, Occupiers and Tenants of Land

Many genealogists and family historians, particularly from outside of the British Isles, are accustomed to using Land Records in their research; yet many record offices and archives in the British Isles appear not to have a separate classification for land records, and many books on British genealogy do not allocate separate chapters to them. This does not mean that there are no records at all referring to owning, purchasing, renting or leasing land - we have already referred to some examples of these in earlier chapters; in fact there are few records which are not, however tenuously, associated with land in some way.

The constituent countries of the British Isles were based on the feudal system whereby all land initially belonged to a sovereign, who shared out various portions or parcels of land to his friends by giving, granting, letting, leasing or selling as his mood or financial situation suited him. Hence the vast majority of British people in the past were tenants, rather than owners of land; which is why many ambitious and adventuresome individuals and families migrated from the British Isles. In the "old country" they would never have had a chance to own their land, or even house; yet in the "new world" they had infinite opportunities, with hard work or money, to own a lot, a plot, a homestead or a farm. Without an established ecclesiastical or manorial system in the New World to record who owned or rented what, this role was undertaken by district, county, state or provincial land registries.

In the British Isles land records have usually been assembled and considered under specialised headings: for example Title Deeds, Manorial Records - the court rolls or registers - Chancery Proceedings, Land Taxes, Maps, Deeds Registries (in Middlesex, Yorkshire and Ireland), Sasines (in Scotland), and Estate Records (in Wales). Glebe Terriers - lists of Church lands - have been mentioned in Chapter 8.

Transfer of ownership, occupancy and tenancy

Do not forget that land (real estate) could be passed on from generation to generation by a will, as we discussed in some detail in Chapter 7; thus probate records are full of references to land. You should also be aware that when marriages took place between couples of any substance arrangements, termed marriage settlements, were usually drawn up in a deed or indenture by which the wife and any children were to be cared for in the event of the husband's death. In many cases the bride's family provided land as part of her dowry. To identify land in your ancestors' time, before map or grid references had been conceived, a parcel of land was described by quoting its size and naming its former owners and occupiers (sometimes giving names of four or more previous individuals), and similarly for adjoining land and adjacent roads and rivers - just the sort of information that you and local historians long for, particularly as individuals' occupations were often included to help uniquely identify them. Marriage settlements, however, were personal documents of the families concerned, not public records; it is only by chance if they have been deposited, often with estate papers, in county or other archives. You will find further information on marriage settlements, dowries (and dower) in the Cameo *Marriage Laws, Rites, Records and Customs.*

Although under the manorial system land may have been owned by the Lord of the Manor - the local squire - it was held under specified conditions by his tenants or vassals; at a sitting of a Manor Court the holding could be renewed. An annual fee, the Common Fine, was payable by the landholder, perhaps an ancestor of yours, at a meeting of the Court Customary, or sometimes the Court Baron. Such a payment, with your ancestor's name, would be recorded in the manor court records or rolls.

As a tenant was given a copy of the record in the manorial register of the conditions of the tenancy of the held land, it became known as copyhold tenure. Persons who held their own land, free from tenancy conditions, owned land by freehold. A later system whereby land could be held under a lease was termed leasehold tenure. If a copyhold tenant died, an heir could apply at a manorial court to take over (in effect inherit) the tenancy - the holding. If the court agreed, the heir's name and occupation were added to the manorial document, after payment of a fee, called a fine. In the early days of the manorial system, when much of the land belonged to the Crown, the tenants were barons. When they died the sovereign, until about 1660, sent out a questionnaire called Questions After Death (*Inquisitiones Post Mortem*, in Latin); this asked how much land the deceased had held, was any rent owing, what was the land worth and who was the previous heir - good genealogical information for you. Whilst the originals, many in the PRO [C132-143, & 145 and E136, & 149-152] are in Latin, many have been transcribed, translated and published by county record, the British Record, and similar societies. County archivists should be able to tell you what is available for their areas. The Manorial Documents Register of the Historical Manuscripts Commission (see Appendix 1) can advise on the whereabouts of manorial records.

Land transfer in Scotland

In Scotland a similar system of transferring land required documents, termed Instruments of Sasine, to be drawn up. These take the form of a Secretary's Register (1599 to 1609) and Registers of Sasines (1617 to 1868), now kept in the National Archives of Scotland. Included in Sasines records are a General Register of Sasines referring to property in any part of Scotland, and Particular Registers for specific parts (counties from 1780) of Scotland. Land in Royal Burghs from 1602 was recorded in separate registers, a few of which are indexed, some in the National Archives, others in regional and district archives. Some Particular Registers to 1780 have published indexes which you can find in a good reference library. The General Register to 1720 is indexed; from 1781 indexed Sasine Abridgements give printed summaries under counties in date order. The indexes are by places to 1830 and from 1872 to the present and also, most usefully for you, by surnames of individuals for all years from 1781. In Scotland, land could also be granted by the Crown under charters of the Great Seal (from 1314, and in Latin until 1651), the Privy Seal (from 1488, also in Latin but in English after 1660) and Signatures (from 1607 to 1847, in English). Most of the volumes of charters in the National Archives have indexes and many have been published. For volumes which are not indexed you will find minutes books useful in discovering individuals. The Signatures indexes provide the name of the grantee, the land, and a reference number to the appropriate land record.

Land ownership disputes

Disputes over land ownership in England and Wales (and inheritance in general) from 1189 were dealt with by the Court of Chancery, whose records are in the PRO [C series]. Many indexes and calendars to these have been published - the Bernau Index (in the Society of Genealogists' Library) to proceedings from 1714 to 1800 is very useful. The Court of Requests, operating from 1485 to 1640, also dealing with land, has surname and place indexes at the PRO [REQ series]. The Court of Common Pleas has Feet of Fines, agreements relating to land ownership in England and Wales, from 1190 to 1838 among its records now in the PRO [CP25]. Many have been transcribed and indexed by record societies.

Land taxes

Taxes have been imposed on land owners and occupiers throughout the British Isles since almost the beginning of time by successive monarchs and governments. Accordingly lists were drawn up of tax payers with their addresses and occupations and the amounts paid. Many thousands of lists have survived. A comprehensive account of surviving British lists is published in the Cameo *Pre-1841 Censuses and Population Listings in the British Isles*. The Cameo gives details of the whereabouts of local and national land tax records from 1086 and highlights and explains important changes in the methods of their collection, such as in 1780. Those who failed to pay their taxes would have been taken to an appropriate court by the landowner in an attempt to recover the money. Thus your ancestors may appear in quarter sessions, manor, borough or similar court records. Valuation Rolls in Scotland from 1855 with names and occupations of owners, tenants and occupiers (but heads of households only), and the value of the property, are in the National Archives of Scotland. These are filed under counties and burghs with some street indexes; persons are not indexed and so your research is less easy. In Scottish Land Court records after 1886 smaller tenancies are identified - and indexed under the names of tenants and crofters. The Sheriffs' court and the local court records are likely to contain references to tenants who failed to pay their rents regularly.

Maps

Maps, whilst not normally categorized as land records, can be useful in tracing your British ancestors, particularly the large-scale early maps as they show fields and field names and the names of tenants and landlords, occupiers and owners. By over 4,700 Private Acts of Parliament, in the form of Inclosure Acts (today often termed

Enclosure Acts) from 1709 and a General Inclosure Act in 1801, many common lands (open fields and forests) and common lands were inclosed. To indicate which parcels of lands were being considered, Inclosure Maps and Awards with names of owners and occupiers were drawn up; many of these maps are now in the PRO or in county archives. There were additionally private inclosure agreements outside the Acts; indeed, from the General Inclosure Act of 1836, inclosure could be achieved by commissioners without a Parliamentary Act. Inclosure was more or less abandoned in the 1870s.

The Tithe Commutation Act of 1836 (there were others to 1860) enabled a clergyman's income (which had been derived previously from a tithe system of produce from land) to be commuted, that is changed, between 1836 and 1842 so that he received an annual rent as a cash sum equivalent. Accordingly from 1838 Tithe Maps and Apportionments were drawn up, also giving names of occupiers. Tithes were abolished altogether in 1936. The Historical Manuscripts Commission can advise you of the present whereabouts of tithe records, although the Map Room at the PRO has a comprehensive collection; many copies are in county and similar archives. The Irish equivalent of the Tithe Commutation Act is described under Deeds Registry - Ireland, below.

The Ordnance Survey was founded in 1791, specifically to map the British Isles on a one inch to one mile scale. Their maps were published from 1805, 110 in the original series and 300 sheets in a new series from 1840. Copies of the original series have been reproduced in recent years and are available commercially. The Curator of Maps at the British Library has a set of the six inch to the mile maps and sells copies - also available from HM Stationary Office. Whilst these do not show names of owners or occupiers, they are useful to indicate towns, villages, hamlets and farms, churches, rivers, hills, canals, roads, and later railways, all of which you will find invaluable in locating the homes of your British ancestors and their possible journeys and migration routes. A series of 25 inches to the mile maps provides much greater detail. Also useful are county and parish maps printed in local histories. A series prepared by the Institute of Heraldic and Genealogical Studies, specifically for ancestor-hunters like yourself, shows the name of every parish in each county and the start date of the earliest parish register. This series is also available bound as *Phillimore's Atlas* having separate indexed tables with notes indicating if the parish registers are on the *IGI* and if other indexes or Nonconformist registers survive.

Maps were also generated as a result of the 1909 Finance Act which initiated a survey by the Inland Revenue of every property in the British Isles. The Maps and associated Field Books, containing names of owners and tenants, if copyhold, freehold or leasehold, the term and rental of the tenancy and a description of the property, are with the Valuation Office records in the PRO [IR121/1 to 135/9]. "Domesday Books", as they are sometimes called, containing names of occupiers were compiled at the same time; these, in many cases with copies of the Valuation Office maps, are in county archives.

Deeds registries - England
In the early 18th Century Deeds Registries were set up for Middlesex (1709) and Yorkshire (West Riding 1704, East Riding and Hull 1708, North Riding 1736). Registers were compiled with descriptions of property and the names and addresses of the interested parties, abstracted from land deeds; the registers are now in the county or comparable archives. Unfortunately this system was not implemented elsewhere in England.

Deeds registry - Ireland
The Registry of Deeds in Ireland was established in 1708 in a specific attempt to ensure that only those loyal to the Established Church (the Anglican Church of Ireland) were granted land. A deed or agreement was drawn up and witnessed between grantor and grantee who had a memorial (copy) made. The memorial was also witnessed by two persons, one of whom was a witness to the original deed. That witness took the memorial to a Justice of the Peace, swore it was a true copy and despatched it to the Registry; there the memorial was retained and transcribed into a registered copy volume. The copy volume was subsequently indexed under grantors (not grantees), although grantees' names, but not the identity of the land before 1833, appear alongside the grantors' in their indexes. The grantors' index after 1833 includes the counties containing the land - which is not necessarily the counties of residence of grantor or grantee. The memorial could take between two days and several (though normally one or two) years to be finally registered. There is a separate Index to Lands by counties and townlands.

In the Registry, besides the main transactions between parties of sales, assignments or conveyances (by lease and release), rent charges, leases and mortgages, there are other records such as probate and marriage settlements which we mentioned earlier. All this material is in the National Archives in Dublin - the deeds for the earliest period being the best preserved and the easiest to read. Those from 1750 to 1840 are particularly useful in genealogical research because names of individuals are amplified by occupations and addresses; thus you can identify your ancestors and discover fascinating details on their lives and property which they either owned or rented from someone else. Many Irish estate records, quite comprehensive but mostly uncatalogued and largely unindexed, dealing with Crown, Landed and Encumbered Estates, and naming lessees and landholders from the late 1500s to the late 1800s, are in the National Library of Ireland, the Irish National Archives and PRONI in Belfast (see Appendix 1).

In Ireland the equivalent of the Tithe Commutation Act was the 1823 Composition Act. Unfortunately for us maps were not drawn and, for a variety of reasons, there were many exemptions; however, Tithe Applotment Books from 1823 to 1838 identify, by townlands within civil parishes, occupiers of land, the area of land and the tithe payable. Another survey, the Primary Valuation of Ireland, was undertaken from 1848 to 1864 by Richard Griffith following the 1842 Tenement Act. This names every householder and landholder in Ireland, identifying, within townlands, from whom each property was leased and the nature of the property (its acreage and value). Neither listings provide genealogical data but in the absence of censuses do identify who was living where in the first half of 19th Century Ireland. Both listings, with modern indexes of surnames for the relevant counties, and either in the National Archives or PRONI, are now available on microfiche in a number of libraries in the English-speaking world and also on CD-ROM.

Estate records - Wales
Welsh Estate rent rolls (rentals), leases and account records, in some aspects, provide you with similar information to that in Customary manorial court rolls; in fact there are some manorial records among Welsh estate papers. After the dissolution of the monasteries considerable tracts of land in Wales passed into the hands of a small number of large landowners. Over the following centuries their number became smaller and their estates larger, mainly as a result of land ownership passing to heiresses who became desirable marriage partners - but who could be wooed only by the wealthy heirs of other land. While through marriage and inheritance Welsh estates grew in size, their small tenants, mostly farming families, remained in place and in many cases passed on their tenancies from one generation to another - similarly to copyhold tenant families we discussed above. Leases for life remained common in south west Wales to the mid-19th Century, even though annual leases had become popular in north Wales. The names and relationships on lease records in the 17th, 18th, and 19th Centuries are even more useful to you than rentals for tracing your Welsh ancestors. Estate surveys from the late 18th Century, when estate owners became more concerned over better management by their stewards and agents, are other useful land records, not only in Wales but elsewhere in the British Isles. Employees on the estates, not necessarily holding land, but house servants, carpenters, grooms and gardeners, were paid regular wages. Many payment account books, with names, perhaps of your ancestors, occupations, wages and dates, have survived. You can easily locate wills and marriage settlements among the Welsh estate papers in the National Library of Wales, as these have been indexed.

By studying a variety of records of Welsh estates you can glean genealogical information on both tenants and landowners - in some cases stretching over 300 years, according to a Land Commission report in the 1890s. From this time the estates began to be sold off in smaller lots, accelerated by the threat of the reintroduction of high land taxes in 1918, the tenants' desires to purchase their holdings and the high prices they were prepared to pay. The estates' sales catalogues - of which there are very many in the National Library of Wales - are other land records you are well advised to consult.

11. Military Records

The Regular and Volunteer Army, Navy and Air Force

Records of the military (the armed forces) are conveniently categorized as:

- before or after the start of the First World War (1914)
- for regular or full-time servicemen and women
- for part-timers and volunteers
- of the army, navy (Royal and Merchant), marines (Royal) or air force (Royal).

As several books have been written on each of these categories, we shall concentrate on records to which you should turn initially when tracing your British ancestors.

Part-time service

The chronicles of crusaders returning to the British Isles in the 12th and 13th Centuries and tales in manorial documents provide us with some of the earliest military records. The concept of Lords of the Manors giving military service to the monarch had its origins in Anglo-Saxon times. Likewise male manorial tenants originally gave military service to their Lord and in return received certain rights and protection. This military service was later commuted to agricultural service or paying a fine (rent), as we discussed in Chapter 10, and the Crown took over the role of calling men into military service when needed. There was no full-time army; a part-time militia was raised as required and those fit to fight or bear arms were identified in each county through surveys, causing militia lists and muster rolls to be drawn up. One of the earliest is for 1297 but by the 16th Century they had become quite common. These lists and rolls are in the PRO and the National Archives of Scotland; several have been transcribed and published. Many of these listings and their background are mentioned in the Cameo *Pre-1841 Censuses and Population Listings in the British Isles*.

The Militia was totally reorganised in England and Wales in 1757 and in Scotland in 1797. Parish constables compiled lists of men from 18 to 50 (the age ranges were altered by later Militia Acts) and forwarded them to a County Lieutenancy. These records, sometimes called Ballot Lists, are most comprehensive for some counties until 1831. The lists contain names, ages, occupations, infirmities and numbers of children under and over 14; later lists contain even more details on individuals. The records which have survived are now in county and similar archives. Supplementary Militias, an Army of Reserves and Local Militias were also formed in 1796, 1803 and 1808 for which further lists, mostly now in the PRO, were compiled. The navy in 1798 also established a militia force, termed the Sea Fencibles, but for local defence only. You will find pay lists for these men from 1798 to 1810 in the ADM28 series at the PRO.

As the fear of a French invasion increased at the end of the 18th Century, Posse Commitatus and Levee en Masse lists were drawn up in 1798 and 1803-4 of able-bodied males between 15 and 60 who were not already involved in military activities - so providing you with further names where you may find an ancestor or two, if the lists have survived. Militia forces did not serve outside the British Isles although during the American Revolution, for example, they spent prolonged periods away from their native counties, often in Ireland. Their families, who remained at home, received an allowance, evidence of which you may discover in a parish record.

After the Napoleonic Wars most militia units were either reorganised or disbanded. From 1831 the Militia comprised only volunteers and new volunteer battalions were formed, linked to full-time county regiments. Such Militia records are in county archives or with the appropriate regimental records, now generally in regimental museum archives (see Appendix 1). The Yeomanry, really mounted volunteers, and the infantry Volunteer Force, were amalgamated with the Militia in 1908 as the Territorial Force. Their records from 1860 to 1912 are in the WO70 series at the PRO.

Records of the Royal Navy Volunteer Reserve to 1919 are in the ADM337 series at the PRO, filed under service numbers obtainable via Medal Rolls (ADM171/125-9).

Full-time service

A full-time military force emerged at the Restoration with the raising of a Standing Army and the formalising of the Navy in 1660 - the recruits receiving better training than had ever been attempted with militiamen. The Marines force was established in 1690 (becoming the Royal Marines in 1802) as a sea service requiring soldiers, rather than sailors. Until 1755 they were administered by the army while on land and by the Admiralty while at sea; thus their records can be found in both WO and ADM series at the PRO.

In both the army and the navy there were commissioned officers, normally men of some substance who bought their commissions, and other ranks (ratings in the navy) whose immediate supervisors were non-commissioned (warrant) officers promoted from the ranks (ratings). A naval officer normally first went to sea as a midshipman - a sort of cadet warrant officer. The records of all these servicemen are in the PRO - which offers some useful leaflets in its *Information Series*. Commissioned officers appear in the annual *Army Lists* in 1740 and from 1754 to the present and in *Navy Lists* from 1782, available in large reference libraries and on the open shelves at the PRO. In 1673 the secular powers wanted assurance that anyone in authority - holding a civil or military office - was committed to the Established Church. Accordingly every such person had to obtain a Sacramental Certificate from a clergyman, churchwardens and two witnesses signifying he had received the eucharist (taken the sacrament of Holy Communion), and lodge the certificate with the Clerk of the Quarter Sessions. You may be able to find a certificate in the county archives for an ancestor of yours. An army of mostly British soldiers was maintained in India by the East India Company until 1859 when the soldiers became part of the British Army. The records prior to 1859 are kept at the British Library, Oriental and India Office Collections, London (see Appendix 1).

Army

To locate an army officer you should use *Army Lists* to find his regiment and then use War Office Registers [WO25], Records of Officers' Services [WO76], Returns with birth, marriage and death certificates [WO42 series] and Registers of baptisms and marriages [WO156] to discover further information. For other army ranks the discharge papers after 1883 are arranged alphabetically for the whole army in Regular Soldiers Discharge Papers [WO97]. Prior to then records are arranged under regiments. If you know the regiment in which your ancestor served before 1883 you can use Discharge Papers or Muster Books and Pay Lists [WO10, 13 & 16]. If you know a place and a date where your ancestor served, you can use Monthly Returns [WO17 & 73] to discover which regiments were stationed there. If you know a particular campaign in which he served you can use Medal Rolls [WO100], to make your search less arduous. Records of Deserters from 1799 to 1852 are in the WO25 series; the civil authorities were encouraged to aid their detection and return by advertisements in the *Police Gazette*, copies of which are in the PRO [HO75/11]. Casualty Lists (1809-57) and Courts Martial (1684-1847) may give you further information on a particular British ancestor. You can read fascinating accounts of army activities in Commanding Officers' log books, now in regimental archives.

Royal Navy

To discover something about your naval commissioned officer ancestor, you should use a similar technique as for an army officer: first locate the man in *Navy Lists* - or in a published naval biography such as O'Byrne or Marshall (see Appendix 2); then turn to Records and Returns of Officers Services from 1660 [ADM9 & 196] with indexes in ADM10. You may find details from 1691 to 1902 on previous service on Lieutenants' Passing Certificates [ADM6, 13 & 107]. Details on Warrant Officers from 1802 to 1871 can be found in their Service Records [ADM29], although some Warrant Officers can be found in Officers' Service Records [ADM196]; you may find additional information in Medical Department Journals from 1785 to 1880 [ADM101] and Registers from 1774 to 1866 [ADM104].

For navy ratings it is advantageous if you know the name of the ship on which your ancestor served between 1667 and 1853 as you can search Ships' Musters [ADM36-39] and Description Books, filed with ships musters if they survive, to piece together his service career. Knowing where and when he served, you could find the ships on that station between 1673 and 1893 by referring to the List Books [ADM8]. A system of Continuous Service Engagement was introduced for seamen from 1853 by which each man was allocated a unique number; details of his date and place of birth were entered in Continuous Service Description Books [ADM139 for 1853-72, and ADM188 for 1873-91]. Brief career information, serving on other ships etc., was added subsequently. Admirals' Journals and Captains', Masters' and Surgeons' logs are in the PRO [ADM50-52 & 101]. Many Lieutenants' logs are in the National Maritime Museum at Greenwich (see Appendix 1).

Royal Marines

Although Marines Officers appear in the Navy Lists, complete records of service before 1793 have not survived. However, you can find some from 1717 in Seniority Lists [ADM118], some from 1760 in Lists of Officers [ADM192] and others from 1777 in the ADM196 series. As with the army and navy, it is easier to trace one of the other ranks in the Marines if you know the division or company of your ancestor. However, there are Description Books from 1750 to 1888 [ADM158] in which individuals are listed alphabetically under the date of their enlistment (attestation); Attestation Forms [ADM157] of individuals from 1790 to 1883 are listed alphabetically within divisions, but annoyingly under their date of discharge from the service.

Royal Air Force

After the invention of aircraft both the army and navy established flying services: the Royal Flying Corps (RFC - formed in 1912) and the Royal Naval Air Service (RNAS - formed in 1914 from the naval wing of the RFC). Their records are in AIR1 & 2 at the PRO. On 1 April 1918 these services were combined into the Royal Air Force (RAF) when a complete muster was taken, the resulting list in numerical order now being in the PRO [AIR10]. An alphabetical index to this will be available.

Air Force Lists, similar in style to those for the other services, have been published annually since 1918. Many RAF records are held by the Ministry of Defence which is releasing material over 30 years old through its Air Historical Branch to the PRO on an annual basis; for example, the records for airmen and non-commissioned officers from 1 April 1918 until the early 1920s are in AIR79. You do not normally have direct access to more recent records; relatives, however, can address queries on officers and airmen (other ranks) to the Personnel Management Centre at Innsworth (see Appendix 1). The Air Historical Branch, having indexes of people, squadrons and aircraft, may also be able to help with limited postal queries. With a prior appointment you can use its comprehensive library.

All ranks of RAF personnel killed in the Second World War are recorded in registers at the Family Records Centre, where you can see the indexes. For further ideas on research in RAF records you should read the PRO booklet (see Appendix 2).

Related to the air service are Airships' log books from 1910 to 1930 which you can find in AIR3 at the PRO.

Other military records

The Registrars General, in addition to civil records of births, marriages and deaths (see Chapter 2), have some Miscellaneous Registers; indexes to English and Welsh persons are available to you at the Family Records Centre. These include Army Chaplains' Registers of Births (1760-1880), of Marriages (1796-1880) and of Deaths (1796-1880), Army Births (1881-1965), Marriages (1881-1965) and Deaths (1880-1965), Army Regimental Registers of Births (1761-1924), and of Deaths (1761-1977), registers of Marriages on HM Ships (1849-1889), and Deaths (1899-

1902) of Field Forces during the wars in South Africa. (The separate series of Army Births, Marriages and Deaths was discontinued after 1965 and if these events took place out of the United Kingdom they appear in Births, Marriages and Deaths Abroad - see Chapter 2.) There is also a larger series of registers of First and Second World War deaths - see below. There are similar registers for Scottish persons in the General Register Office in Edinburgh, namely Army Returns of births, marriages and deaths (1881-1959), Service Department Registers (from 1959) and Army Chaplains' registers of marriages (from 1892) if at least one party was Scottish and one was in British military service.

Army records from 1914, particularly during the First and Second World Wars (1914-18 and 1939-45) were originally voluminous. Unfortunately very many First World War ("The Kaiser's War") records were destroyed by enemy action in the Second World War ("Hitler's War"). Nevertheless, official records which survived (some in a much damaged state), are being passed, together with much other military material, to the PRO where they are being microfilmed and gradually being made available for public research. You can use many other records and lists of military personnel who were awarded medals, wounded or killed in both World Wars. Some lists are now in the PRO or regimental archives, others have been published by the Stationery Office (HMSO) or by local firms commemorating local heroes.

Medals Rolls with indexes are in the PRO [WO239], official War Office Weekly Casualty Lists from 7 August 1917 are in the British Library Newspaper Library at Colindale (see Appendix 1) and an 81 volume *Soldiers in the Great War* has been reprinted in regimental volumes, available in many libraries, now also on CD-ROM. County archives and local libraries have much material on local people involved in the World Wars. The Wellcome Historical Medical Library has published two fascinating volumes on *Commissioned Officers in the Medical Services of the British Army 1660-1960*, while the Navy Records Society has compiled details on *Commissioned Sea Officers of the Royal Navy, 1660-1815* (see Appendix 2).

The Commonwealth War Graves Commission (see Appendix 1) tends the graves of the dead from the former British Empire and British Commonwealth in beautifully maintained cemeteries around the world. For a fee they can provide details on the location of individual graves, regiments and sometimes corps and next of kin. The same details, held on the Debt of Honour Register, are available from their website <http://www.cwgc.org>, which also offers some interesting information on each cemetery and the relevant conflicts. The Imperial War Museum in London (website address <http://www.iwm.org.uk>) (also see Appendix 1) co-ordinates a National Inventory of War Memorials project, to record details from local memorials in city squares, village greens, factories and town halls, throughout the British Isles, apart from the Republic of Ireland. You can consult the following separate Registrar General's War Death Indexes for 1914-21 and for 1939-45 at the Family Records Centre: Army Officers, Army Other Ranks, Navy Officers, Navy Other Ranks.

Scottish persons are recorded in similar registers at the General Register Office in Edinburgh.

The Imperial War Museum is well worth a visit for military information from 1812; there is an extensive library of books and photographs which you can use by prior appointment. You do not need to make an appointment for the library at the National Army Museum in Chelsea (see Appendix 1).

Related services
Merchant Seamen were not part of the military establishment, although in times of crises they and their vessels were called into service. For details on these seamen and their records, in the PRO [BT series], you should read the PRO publication by K Smith, CT Watts and MJ Watts (see Appendix 2).

Whilst also not military personnel, this is a convenient place to say that if your ancestor was a coastguard in the British Isles, the Muster Books from 1824 to 1857 and the Records of Service from 1816 to 1923 are in the Admiralty records [ADM119 & 175] at the PRO.

The Royal National Lifeboat Institution (RNLI) was established in 1824 as a volunteer organisation to rescue persons from vessels in distress around the British Isles. Records of individuals and events are maintained at its headquarters in West Quay Road, Poole, BH15 1HS; the RNLI small library is open to the public.

Records of lighthouse and lightship keepers around England, Wales, Gibraltar and the Channel Islands began after the Corporation of Trinity House (see Appendix 1) built its first lighthouse in 1609. Regrettably all pre-1900 records were largely destroyed in 1666, 1714 and by enemy bombing in 1940. Fortunately, however, the requests (petitions) from disabled lightkeepers and seamen (mostly the latter), and their widows and orphans, for assistance from the Trinity House charities from 1787 to 1854 had been deposited with the Society of Genealogists in 1934; individuals' names on these petitions were indexed and published in 1990. As a result of remote operation and automation, lightkeepers ceased to be recruited by Trinity House in 1980. Records of lightkeepers around Scotland and the Isle of Man were kept by the Northern Lighthouse Board in Edinburgh and are now in the National Archives of Scotland; included are Board minutes from 1786, staff records, registers and lists of lightkeepers, 1837-1980 (but closed to the public for 30 years), lighthouse visitors' albums from 1854 and shipwreck returns, 1824-1983. There are also records from individual lighthouses and some 700 volumes of correspondence from January 1900 to the present. The lighthouses around all of Ireland were successively under the care of the Commissioners for Barracks (from 1767), the Revenue Board, the Ballast Board (from 1810) and the Commission of Irish Lights (since 1867). Their records are not indexed and are less voluminous than those for the Northern Lighthouse Board, but they do contain many names of lightkeepers; the Commission, at 16 Lower Pembroke Street, Dublin 2, is prepared to help enquirers wherever possible.

12. Family History Societies

The Federation and its Member Societies

Family Historians and genealogists enjoy getting together. As a county or regional archive is a focal point for research in many parts of the British Isles, Family History Societies have been formed and organised in each county or region, often based in the town or city where the archives are situated. In some counties there is more than one Society and some local Societies have several branch groups in their area. Most Societies were founded by volunteers and generally receive no financial funding from central or local government.

The majority of the Family History Societies hold meetings once a month at which an invited lecturer or a member speaks on a specific aspect of historical or genealogical research. Each Society also publishes its own Journal or Magazine, usually once every three months; these "Quarterlies" typically contain articles written by the members themselves on research techniques, local topography, specific families, parishes and archives. Most Journals also announce the dates, lecture titles and venues for their monthly meetings and they publish surnames which the individual members of that Society are researching - so providing information which members can share between themselves to help each other in tracing their ancestors. Some Societies, usually in conjunction with other groups, organise Open Days or Family History Fairs from time to time at which indexes and transcripts are available and genealogical products, maps, postcards and books can be purchased from local and national bodies.

Most local Family History Societies have three groups of members: in the first group are those whose ancestors originated in the locality but they, the descendants, now live away - many huge distances from the British Isles. These members would not normally be able to attend the Society meetings but they are able to maintain contact by receiving the Journal regularly. In the second group are those who live in the locality but whose ancestors lived elsewhere. They have joined the Society because they can attend the monthly meetings and so learn from the lectures and enjoy the fellowship with other members at the meeting. In the third group - generally the smallest but the most fortunate - are those who live today in the same locality as their ancestors formerly did; not only can people in this group attend the monthly meetings but they have easy access to the archives where details of their ancestors are waiting to be discovered.

County and similar Family History Societies thus encourage their members to enjoy their own ancestral research yet in an organised and logical manner. To enable this to be undertaken more easily and also to secure historical information for future generations, most Societies are also engaged in corporate projects. The four most popular are the transcription and indexing of (a) inscriptions on tombstones in graveyards and cemeteries in their area; (b) Church marriage registers in their area from 1800 (or earlier) to 1837 (when civil registration of births, marriages and deaths began in England and Wales - see Chapter 2); (c) burial registers; (d) 19th Century civil census returns. The very successful 1881 census project, in which most Member Societies participated, was completed in 1996 and the resulting transcribed returns and indexes made available on microfiche and CD-ROM. The National Burial Index is another joint project, in this instance burial entries from parish and nonconformist registers, providing a nation-wide database, to complement the IGI which comprises mostly baptisms and marriages.

The activities of most of the above Societies are co-ordinated by the Federation of Family History Societies which was founded in 1974 and is now based in Birmingham, England, telephone 07041-492032. You may more conveniently find the details you need on the Federation's website at <http://www.ffhs.org.uk>. For the postal address see Appendix 1. The Federation's role encompasses Education, Projects, Public Affairs and Publishing. The co-ordination of Societies in Scotland is undertaken by the Scottish Association of Family History Societies (see Appendix 1). For convenient operation the Federation, registered as a charity with the British Charity Commission, was reformed in 1995 into a Company, Limited by Guarantee. The Federation, acting on behalf of the thousands of members of its Member Societies, has representation on several national advisory bodies which are interested in the preservation and accessibility of British archival records.

The Federation is owned by its constituent Societies and so has no individual members. Business meetings are held at different venues in the British Isles every April and September, the Annual General Meeting taking place in conjunction with the April meeting. To all these meetings a representative from every Member Society is invited, thus comprising the Federation Council. The representatives at the Annual General Meeting elect the Chairman and Treasurer and other Directors who together comprise an Executive Committee, responsible for the organisation and operation of the Federation. Members of this Committee act as the Charity's Board of Directors and (for Charity Law purposes) its Trustees. The Committee members are unpaid volunteers although the Federation has some paid part-time employees.

Most meetings of the Federation Council take place during a weekend conference hosted by one of its Member Societies; at any of these conferences you as a family historian would be welcome to spend two or three days immersed in lectures and discussions on a variety of genealogical topics, in a scholarly and yet friendly and enjoyable atmosphere.

In addition to the geographically-based Societies, there are others whose members are all researching one particular surname - conducting a one-name study. Some of these Societies have many members, produce regular publications and hold meetings similarly to the county Societies; others are considerably smaller, really individuals, but holding vast amounts of data on the surname in which they are interested. Most of these Societies and well-organised individuals belong to the Guild of One-Name

Studies (GOONS). You can write to the Guild at the address given in Appendix 1 for a list of their registered members or look at its website on the Internet at: <http://www.one-name.org>.

Another group of Member Societies of the Federation comprises those having a particular topic interest such as a denomination or religion or links with a particular country or section of the community; for example Catholic, Jewish, Huguenot, Anglo-French, Anglo-German and Gypsy and Romany families. Details of these Societies can be obtained form the Federation's Administrator or from the website mentioned earlier in this chapter.

Also belonging to the Federation are genealogical and family history societies based outside of the British Isles but having a significant number of members with British ancestors. These individuals (perhaps you are one of them) are thus able to become better informed about British archives and genealogical research through the association of their Societies with the Federation. The Federation's Administrator, or the website (see above), can give you information on these societies. In addition many Member Societies around the world exchange their quarterly Journals or Magazines with those of other Member Societies and accordingly publicise their activities.

The Federation publishes *Family History News & Digest* to coincide with the six-monthly conferences. Besides containing news on British national and local record offices and archives and details of the activities of its Member Societies, it has an extremely useful central digest section with indexed abstracts from articles recently published on relevant research on genealogy, family history and heraldry. In addition, the latest list of the Member Societies of the Federation and the addresses of their honorary secretaries are included, although these are also available on the Internet, as identified above. Member Societies with e-mail addresses can also be found at <http://www.Hawgood.co.uk/ffhs.htm>. Each Member Society receives a complimentary copy of *Family History News & Digest* but it may be purchased by individuals such as yourself.

The Federation owns a subsidiary company, FFHS (Publications) Ltd., offering an extensive range of low-priced booklets on a variety of aspects of British family history and genealogical research, some of which are identified in Appendix 2; these are available from the company (for the address see Appendix 1) or through the Member Societies of the Federation.

13. Heraldry

Your ancestors and their armigerous contacts

Do not ignore this chapter, or join most family historians and many genealogists who keep, quite unnecessarily, right away from heraldry. Maybe you have discovered from the 19th Century censuses (see Chapter 5) that your ancestors were "Ag.Lab." - agricultural labourers; then in a parish register (see Chapter 6) you have seen "pauper" written against an ancestor's burial entry; and to top it all, there in the poor law documentation (see Chapter 9) is the same family being examined by a magistrate, about to be removed by the constable to their former home because they have become a burden to their adopted parish. By now you believe that such ancestors can surely never have been entitled to a coat of arms.

However, to shy away from heraldry is unwise for two reasons: firstly, families rarely remained in the same social class for more than a few generations - "upwards and downwards mobility", the experts call it; secondly, even if your ancestors always DO seem to have been someone else's workers or servants or faithful tenants, it is quite likely that their masters were armigerous (had coats of arms). Very often when someone of substance moved from one part of the country to another, they took their retinue with them. And so by tracking the movements of the armigers, you may be able to follow the movements of their faithful staff - your ancestors. It is useful, therefore, if you have some understanding of heraldry and of how grants of arms were awarded and the circumstances under which the personal achievement of one person could be inherited by another.

Space does not permit us to describe here more than the fundamentals of heraldry. There are several books that cover the subject at length. However, it is important for you to appreciate that the heralds at the College of Arms in London, whose activities are co-ordinated by Garter King-of-Arms in England and Wales (Lyon King-of-Arms is chief herald in Scotland, Ulster King-of-Arms is chief herald in Ireland), in effect report through the Earl Marshal to the monarch. Incidentally, though nothing to do with heraldry, you may be able to find an ancestor, including heralds, employed directly by the monarch in the Royal Archives at Windsor (see Appendix 1). In the past, monarchs awarded coats of arms (granted armorial achievements) to individuals for favours and services rendered to the Crown. Arms can also be granted to corporate bodies, towns and institutions, and can be purchased by individuals and bodies who meet certain criteria.

The heralds were, and are, experts in interpreting who is entitled to which coat of arms and on guiding individuals in the composition of their armorial achievements. The heralds advise which design to have on a shield (the charges on the field, how it should be divided or parted and the tinctures - notice that we have not said colours). Some designs take advantage or make fun of suitable surnames (this is called canting): Thomas Pleys, for example, could have a yellow fish (plaice) - the charge -

on a blue background - the field. The tinctures used are categorized as metals, colours and furs: the metals are *argent* (silver) which appears white, and *or* (gold) which appears yellow; the colours are *rouge* (red), *azure* (blue), *vert* (green), *purpure* (purple) and *sable* (black); occasionally *tenne* (tawny brown) and *sanguine* or *murrey* (mulberry) are included. The common furs are *ermine* and *vair* but *ermines, erminois, pean, counter-vair, potent* and *counter-potent* are also used.

There are strict rules of tincture adhered to by the heralds: no coloured charge may appear on a coloured field, no metal on a metal and no fur on a fur. That is why the yellow (a metal) fish would be correctly depicted on a blue (a colour) field, and could not be shown on a white (another metal) field. Under very specific circumstances, and having demonstrated a proven genealogy, the heralds permit a child to use an almost identical coat of arms as the armigerous parent, but bearing a small mark of difference, a cadency mark, on top of the parent's design.

Over the centuries a number of unscrupulous individuals "assumed" armorial achievements that they had devised themselves, without any reference to the heralds at the College of Arms; or they simply used a coat of arms that had been granted to another individual, sometimes having the same surname, but being no relative at all. Not infrequently the descendants of these rogues "inherited" the illegally assumed arms. As a check on who was using what, or claiming to be descended from whom, the heralds from 1530 until 1686 occasionally went on Visitations or tours around the counties of the country. They made notes and sketches of arms and drew up pedigree charts and family trees, reprimanding those who were abusing the system.

The Harleian Society and others have abstracted and published on a county basis some of the results of the Heralds Visitations, with illustrations of the coats of arms and the accompanying genealogies. In some cases the pedigrees cover many generations and indicate when an individual or branch of a family moved from one area to another. You, therefore, should look at these printed Visitation records, in case you discover similar migration patterns for your ancestors. You may, of course, find your own ancestors named in these volumes, in which case you will be pleased that you expressed an interest in heraldry. You can see the publications of the Harleian Society and similar bodies in some large reference libraries.

Marshalling of arms, the system by which a child combined both parents' armorial achievements into a new design, but with the originals clearly recognizable, is an important aspect where heraldry pictorially shows genealogical descent. Inheriting an armorial achievement was usually associated with inheriting property; and acquiring property was a symbol of wealth or social status. Hence a complicated achievement, resulting from marshalling, could indicate an individual of some standing. If you have found a complex coat of arms borne by one of your ancestors, that could mean that you are descended from a person of note - or perhaps a person who found a mischievous herald or an heraldic artist with a love for ornamentation.

14. Your Formal Family History

Organising and writing it all up

Now that you have enjoyed the previous chapters of this Cameo, you will have collected masses of information on your ancestors - and perhaps you are wondering how to handle it all - or even why you began to trace your British ancestors.

Having made the acquaintance of all (or even some) of your ancestors, what do you do with them? Hopefully you will have dipped into this chapter before trying all the sources in the earlier chapters. Otherwise, as we suspected earlier, you are now beginning to disappear under collections of charts, piles of papers, boxes of binders and hundreds of photographs (are they all identified?) and photocopies falling out of files in what used to be a tidy room - or a tidy house. Or perhaps you have data on a variety of floppy diskettes or on your hard disk and you are still wondering which genealogical package or family tree program you ought to use.

By now you should have decided who you are tracing: all those ancestors from whom you are descended - 2 parents, 4 grandparents, 8 great-grandparents, 16, 32, 64.....to 1,048,576 of them 20 generations ago or 33,554,432 of them 25 generations ago (assuming 25 years per generation, this means that you had 33 ½ million direct ancestors 625 years ago - if there was no inter-marrying of cousins, or anyone else!); or perhaps you are tracing only the female line (at least you can be sure of that one); or maybe you are tracing only your surname back; or even doing a one-name study - collecting every reference to one surname - incidentally, did you join the Guild of One-Name Studies (see Chapter 12)?

Many genealogists believe that all of their problems would be solved if they had a good filing system. Not so. Many years ago I had a secretary who had a good filing system. I had the perfect office - not a scrap of paper to be seen, no heaps in the in-tray, nothing pending, everything filed away. But when I wanted a particular file it took hours, sometimes days, to find it. The filing was fine, but the system of retrieval was at fault. And so I advocate that you develop a good retrieval system for all your genealogical data and family history documents and files.

Whether you use paper or have that microfilmed and store your information in microform or perhaps use a computer is immaterial. Give each file a title, label it, put it in a logical place, and make a note of where you have put it so that you can find it again. You should also consider explaining your filing and retrieval system to another member of your family or a friend, in case something should happen to you and all your efforts remain inaccessible to others for ever. Some people have huge master family tree charts, giving every ancestor an identifier - reference numbers or letters - and then separately file details on each individual by those identifiers, or alphabetically or chronologically by birthdates. Some people have their principal families colour-coded, putting family members in files under those colours. Some people use suspension files in cabinets, some use cards in drawers (or even shoe boxes), some use A4-size or letter-size binders on shelves, others use box files. Some people keep their photographs in separate and acid-free envelopes, labelled on the outside, with documents relating to the individuals, others have separate photo-albums cross-referenced to other files. Some people attempt to put everything on computers and store all their data on floppy diskettes or even CD-ROM - which is now practicable as scanners and suitable software packages become more accessible. Some people have mixtures of all these.

There is no "correct" way to file your accumulated collection of certificates, charts, photographs and notes. Some photocopies fade with time, others stick together and some paper deteriorates. But the people in your documents are your ancestors, from your family, and so you are entitled to arrange the details for your convenience. Be aware of the potential dangers of having only one copy of all your research results in one place. A friend of mine had been tracing her ancestry for 25 years and kept all her files in one room of her house - which was burned to the ground when she was away. Her insurance covered the cost of the papers and disks on which 25 years of work were stored - but the work itself was lost for ever. Since then I have persuaded a relative, several miles from where I keep my own materials, to house a complete copy of my files. Some of us do not have 25 years left in which to repeat all the research, and some of the sources used have disappeared anyway.

This is not the place to recommend a particular computer database or program for sorting and assembling your genealogy, nor yet a computer or printer on which to compile and print out pedigree charts and the like. There are enough shareware and commercial and personalized programs on the market, and reviews of them, for you to make your choice. Many computer groups within family history and genealogical societies can advise you and there are several genealogical computing magazines. Make some contacts, find out who has copies of which programs and ask if you can try them out on their computers before you finally decide. Just like the paper filing systems, you should choose a system or program that you are happy to use and are comfortable with.

Now that you have traced some of your British ancestors and assembled loads of facts on them, and filed them in ways such that you can instantly recover them all, you should seriously consider writing up your family history, perhaps even publishing it. Do not wait until you have finished doing your research before you start writing - you will never totally complete your hunt, so you will never get around to writing it up for future generations to enjoy the results of your labours.

Never compile a textbook full of pedigree charts of names and mere dates; that will not inspire anyone, especially the present members of your family who are, as yet, unconvinced that tracing ancestors is a sane pastime. Choose a narrative style that will make interesting reading, a story about the lives and times of your ancestors. Include some contemporary local and national events, possibly the names of the reigning monarch and the local clergyman - you do not live in a vacuum, and neither did your ancestors; yet so many family histories imply that the family in question was the only one in the universe at the time. The types of book that we mentioned in Chapter 4 will be of use to you again at this point, to provide a scene into which to set your ancestors.

And having finished your first family history, have a look at some specialised books on British social, economic and church history and their records, from where you can collect further material for your second. Or you can collect some friends together, share your experiences and tell them how they also can trace their British ancestors.

Appendix 1

Useful Addresses

Civil Registration

Public Search Rooms:
Family Records Centre,
(GRO), Ground Floor,
1 Myddelton Street, Islington,
London, EC1R 1UW.

Registrar General,
Joyce House,
8-11 Lombard Street East,
Dublin 2,
Republic of Ireland.

*Postal Applications for English and
Welsh certificates:*
ONS, General Register Office,
PO Box 2,
Southport,
Merseyside, PR8 2JD.

Civil Registry,
Deemster's Walk,
Bucks Road,
Douglas,
Isle of Man, IM1 3AR.

Registrar General,
New Register House,
Princes Street,
Edinburgh, EH1 3YT,
Scotland.

Registrar General,
The Greffe,
Royal Court House,
St Peter Port, Guernsey,
Channel Islands, GY1 2PB.

Registrar General,
Oxford House,
49-55 Chichester Street,
Belfast, BT1 4HL,
Northern Ireland.

Superintendent Registrar,
States Office,
Royal Square,
St Helier, Jersey,
Channel Islands, JE2 4WA.

Civil Probate Registries

Principal Registry of the Family Division,
First Avenue House,
42-49 High Holborn,
London, WC1V 6NP.

Irish Testamentary Court,
Registry of Deeds,
Henrietta Street,
Dublin 1.

National & Regional Archives & Libraries

Public Record Office,
Ruskin Avenue, Kew,
Surrey, TW9 4DU.

National Archives of Scotland,
HM General Register House,
Edinburgh, EH1 3YY.

Censuses etc. in microform;
Family Records Centre,
(PRO), First Floor,
1 Myddelton Street,
Islington,
London, EC1R 1UW.

Public Record Office of Northern Ireland,
66 Balmoral Avenue,
Belfast, BT9 6NY.

Irish National Archives,
Bishop Street,
Dublin 8, Republic of Ireland.

British Library,
76 Euston Road,
London NW1 2DB.

British Library Newspaper Library,
Colindale Avenue,
London, NW9 5HE.

Guildhall Library,
Aldermanbury,
London, EC2 2EJ.

Historical Manuscripts Commission,
Quality Court,
Chancery Lane,
London, WC2A 1HP.

National Library of Wales,
Aberystwyth,
Ceredigion, SY23 3BU.

National Library of Scotland,
George IV Bridge,
Edinburgh, EH1 1EW.

National Library of Ireland,
Kildare Street,
Dublin 2,
Republic of Ireland.

Manx Museum Library,
Kingswood Grove,
Douglas,
Isle of Man, IM1 3LY.

Priaulx Library,
Candie,
St Peter Port, Guernsey,
Channel Islands, GY1 1UG.

La Société Guernesiaise,
Lucis House, The Grange,
St Peter Port, Guernsey,
Channel Islands, GY1 2QG.

La Société Jersiaise,
7 Pier Road,
St Helier, Jersey,
Channel Islands, JE2 4UW.

Specialist Collections

Lambeth Palace Library,
London, SE1 7JU.

Borthwick Institute of Historical Research,
St Anthony Hall,
York, YO1 2PW.

Ecclesiastical Court Dean,
12 New Street,
St Peter Port, Guernsey,
Channel Islands, GY1 2PF.

College of Arms,
Queen Victoria Street,
London, EC4V 4BT.

Royal Archives,
Windsor Castle,
Windsor,
Berkshire, SL4 1NJ.

House of Lords Record Office,
London, SW1A 0PN.

Trinity College,
College Street,
Dublin 2.

Royal Irish Academy,
19 Dawson Street,
Dublin 2.

Denominational Archives

Catholic Record Society,
114 Mount Street,
London, W1X 6AX.

Friends Library,
173 Euston Road,
London, NW1 2BJ.

Baptist Union,
129 Broadway, Didcot,
Oxfordshire, OX11 8XA.

Jewish Historical Society,
33 Seymour Place,
London, W1H 5AP.

United Reformed Church Hist. Soc. & Libry.,
Westminster College, Madingley Road,
Cambridge, CB3 0AA.
(Congregational and Presbyterian records)

Methodist Connexional Archivist,
Central Hall, Oldham Street,
Manchester, M1 1JQ.

Huguenot Society,
University College,
Gower Street,
London, WC1E 6BT.

Dr Williams's Library,
14 Gordon Square,
London, WC1H 0AG.

Military and Related Records

Imperial War Museum,
Lambeth Road,
London, SE1 6HZ.

National Army Museum,
Royal Hospital Road,
London, SW3 4HT.

National Maritime Museum,
Romney Road, Greenwich,
London, SE10 9NF.

Air Historical Branch (MOD),
3-5 Great Scotland Yard,
London, SW1A 2HW.

RAF Personnel Management Centre,
PM(AR1b), [for Officers] or
P/Man 3D, [for Airmen]
Innsworth,
Gloucestershire, GL3 1EZ.

Commonwealth War Graves Commission,
2 Marlow Road,
Maidenhead,
Berkshire, SL6 7DX.

Trinity House,.
Tower Hill,
London, EC3N 4DH.
(English & Welsh Lighthouse Keepers)

Family History & Genealogical Organisations

Federation of Family History Societies,
Birmingham and Midland Institute,
Margaret Street,
Birmingham, B3 3BS.
Tel: 07041-492032.

FFHS (Publications) Ltd.,
2-4 Killer Street,
Ramsbottom, Bury
Lancashire, BL0 9BZ.

Scottish Association of Family History Societies,
51/3 Mortonhall Road,
Edinburgh, EH9 2HN,
Scotland.

Society of Genealogists,
14 Charterhouse Buildings,
Goswell Road,
London, EC1M 7BA.

Institute of Heraldic and Genealogical Studies,
80 Northgate,
Canterbury,
Kent, CT1 1BA.

Guild of One Name Studies,
Box G,
14 Charterhouse Buildings,
Goswell Road,
London, EC1M 7BA.

Genealogical Publications

Family Tree Magazine
61 Great Whyte,
Ramsey, Peterborough,
PE17 1HL.

Family History Monthly,
45 St Mary's Road,
Ealing,
London, W5 5RQ.

Appendix 2
Further Reading

Baxter, I A. *A Brief Guide to Biographical Sources (in the India Office Library)*. British Library. 1990.

Brooke-Little, J P. *Boutell's Heraldry*. Warne. 1978.

Chapman, Colin R. *Pre-1841 Census & Population Listings in the British Isles*. Lochin Publishing. 5th edn 1998.

Chapman, Colin R. *The Growth of British Education & Its Records*. Lochin Publishing. 2nd edn 1994.

Chapman, Colin R. *Ecclesiastical Courts, Officials & Records: Sin, Sex & Probate*. Lochin Publishing. 2nd edn 1997.

Chapman, Colin R. *How Heavy, How Much & How Long?* Lochin Publishing. 1999.

Chapman, Colin R with Litton, Pauline. *Marriage Laws, Rites, Records & Customs*. Lochin Publishing. 1996.

Chapman, Colin R. *Tracing Ancestors in Bedfordshire*. Lochin Publishing. 2nd edn 1998.

Chapman, Colin R. *Tracing Ancestors in Northamptonshire*. Lochin Publishing. 3rd edn 1999.

Chapman, Colin R. *Tracing Ancestors in Rutland*. Lochin Publishing. 1997.

Chapman, Colin R. *They Removed My Poor Ancestors*. Lochin Publishing. [being revised.]

Chapman, Colin R. *An Introduction to Using Newspapers & Periodicals*. FFHS. 2nd edn 1996.

Cole, J & Church, R. *In and Around Record Repositories in Great Britain and Ireland*. ABM Publishing. 4th edn 1998.

Conyers-Nesbit, R. et al. *RAF Records in the PRO*. PRO. 1994

Drew, R. *Commissioned Officers in the Medical Services of the British Army. Vol.2, 1898-1960*. Wellcome Historical Medical Library. 1968.

Eden, F M. *The State of the Poor*. London. 1797.

[Family Welfare Association]. *Charities Digest*. Waterlow. An annual publication.

[FFHS]. *Current Publications by Member Societies*. FFHS. 8th edn 1996.

Fowler, S; revised by Spencer, W. *Army Records for Family Historians*. PRO. 1998.

Gibson, J. & Hampson, E. *Marriage and Census Indexes*. FFHS. 7th edn 1998.

Gibson, J. & Hampson, E. *Specialist Indexes for Family Historians*. FFHS. 1998.

Gibson, J. *Probate Records - Where to look for Wills*. FFHS. 4th edn 1997.

Gibson, J. & Peskett, P. *Record Offices: How to Find Them*. FFHS. 8th edn 1998.

Gibson, J S W (et al). *Poor Law Union Records*. (4 vols). FFHS. 1993, 1997.

Holding, N. *The Location of British Army Records 1914-1918*. FFHS. 1999.

Humphery-Smith, C R. *Phillimore Atlas and Index of Parish Registers*. Phillimore. 1995.

Marshall, J. *Royal Naval Biography*. London. 1823-30.

O'Byrne, W R. *A Naval Biographical Dictionary*. London. 1849.

Pelling, George. *Beginning Your Family History*. Revised by Litton, Pauline. FFHS. 1998.

Peterkin, A & Johnston, W. *Commissioned Officers in the Medical services of the British Army. 2 Vols., 1660-1960*. Wellcome Historical Medical Library. 1968.

Raymond, S A. *A Genealogical Bibliography*. (many vols). FFHS. 1992+.

Richardson, J. *The Local Historian's Encyclopaedia*. Historical Publications. 1986.

Saul, Pauline. *The Family Historian's Enquire Within*. FFHS. 1997.

Smith, K., Watts, C T & M J. *Records of Merchant Shipping & Seaman*. PRO. 1998.

Steel, D J. *Family History in Focus*. Lutterworth Press. 1984.

Syrett, D & DiNardo, R L. *Commissioned Sea Officers of the Royal Navy 1660-1815*. Scolar. 1994.

Tate, W E. *The Parish Chest*. Phillimore. 1996.

Watts, M J & C T. *My Ancestor was in the British Army*. SoG. 1995.

Wise, Terence. *A Guide to Military Museums*. Athena Books. 1986.

Family Tree Magazine. (a regular publication).

Family History Monthly. (a regular publication).

Index